JUDGING CIVIL JUSTICE

The civil justice system supports social order and economic activity, but a number of factors over the last decade have created a situation in which the value of civil justice is being undermined and the civil courts are in a state of dilapidation.

For the 2008 Hamlyn Lectures, Dame Hazel Genn discusses reforms to civil justice in England and around the world over the last decade in the context of escalating expenditure on criminal justice and vanishing civil trials. In critically assessing the claims and practice of mediation for civil disputes, she questions whether diverting cases out of the public courts and into private dispute resolution promotes access to justice, looks critically at the changed expectations of the judiciary in civil justice and points to the need for a better understanding of how judges 'do justice'.

DAME HAZEL GENN is Dean of Laws, Professor of Socio-Legal Studies and Co-director of the Centre for Empirical Legal Studies in the Faculty of Laws at University College London, where she is also an Honorary Fellow. In 2006, she was appointed an Inaugural Commissioner of the new Judicial Appointments Commission, established under the Constitutional Reform Act 2005. She was also a member of the Committee on Standards in Public Life from 2003 to 2008. She worked with the Judicial Studies Board for twelve years, serving as a member of the main board and the tribunals committee, closely involved in the design and delivery of training for the judiciary at all levels. A leading authority on access to justice, she has published widely in the field.

JUDGING CIVIL JUSTICE

HAZEL GENN

CAMBRIDGE
UNIVERSITY PRESS

CAMBRIDGE UNIVERSITY PRESS
Cambridge, New York, Melbourne, Madrid, Cape Town, Singapore,
São Paulo, Delhi, Dubai, Tokyo

Cambridge University Press
The Edinburgh Building, Cambridge CB2 8RU, UK

Published in the United States of America by Cambridge University Press, New York

www.cambridge.org
Information on this title: www.cambridge.org/9780521118941

First published 2010

Printed in the United Kingdom at the University Press, Cambridge

A catalogue record for this publication is available from the British Library

Library of Congress Cataloguing in Publication data
Genn, Hazel G.
    Judging civil justice / Hazel Genn.
        p.   cm.
    ISBN 978-0-521-11894-1 (Hardback)
    1. Justice, Administration of–England.   I. Title.
    KD7100.G46 2010
    347.42–dc22   2009029829

ISBN 978-0-521-11894-1 Hardback
ISBN 978-0-521-13439-2 Paperback

In memory of my dear sisters
Rosemary and Angela

CONTENTS

vii

The Hamlyn Trust owes its existence today to the will of the late Miss Emma Warburton Hamlyn of Torquay, who died in 1941 at the age of 80. She came of an old and well-known Devon family. Her father, William Bussell Hamlyn, practised in Torquay as a solicitor and JP for many years, and it seems likely that Miss Hamlyn founded the trust in his memory. Emma Hamlyn was a woman of strong character, intelligent and cultured, well versed in literature, music and art, and a lover of her country. She travelled extensively in Europe and Egypt, and apparently took considerable interest in the law and ethnology of the countries and cultures that she visited. An account of Miss Hamlyn by Professor Chantal Stebbings of the University of Exeter may be found, under the title 'The Hamlyn Legacy', in volume 42 of the published lectures.

Miss Hamlyn bequeathed the residue of her estate on trust in terms which it seems were her own. The wording was thought to be vague, and the will was taken to the Chancery Division of the High Court, which in November 1948 approved a Scheme for the administration of the trust. Paragraph 3 of the Scheme, which follows Miss Hamlyn's own wording, is as below:

> The object of the charity is the furtherance by lectures or otherwise among the Common People of the United Kingdom of Great Britain and Northern Ireland of

the knowledge of the Comparative Jurisprudence and Ethnology of the Chief European countries including the United Kingdom, and the circumstances of the growth of such jurisprudence to the Intent that the Common People of the United Kingdom may realise the privileges which in law and custom they enjoy in comparison with other European Peoples and realising and appreciating such privileges may recognise the responsibilities and obligations attaching to them.

The Trustees are to include the Vice-Chancellor of the University of Exeter, representatives of the Universities of London, Leeds, Glasgow, Belfast and Wales and persons co-opted. At present there are eight Trustees:

Professor N. Burrows, The University of Glasgow
Professor I.R. Davies, Swansea University
Ms Clare Dyer
Professor K.M. Economides [representing the Vice-Chancellor of the University of Exeter] (Chairman)
Professor R. Halson, University of Leeds
Professor J. Morison, Queen's University, Belfast
The Rt Hon. Lord Justice Sedley
Professor A. Sherr, University of London
Clerk; Ms Sarah Roberts, University of Exeter

From the outset it was decided that the objects of the Trust could be best achieved by means of an annual course of public lectures of outstanding interest and quality by eminent lecturers, and by their subsequent publication and distribution to a wider audience. The first of the Lectures were delivered by the Rt Hon. Lord Justice Denning (as he then was) in 1949. Since then there has been an unbroken series of annual Lectures published until 2005 by Sweet & Maxwell and from 2006 by Cambridge University Press. A complete list of the Lectures may be found on pages xii to xiv. In 2005 the Trustees decided to supplement the Lectures with an annual Hamlyn Seminar, normally held at the Institute of Advanced Legal Studies at the University of London, to mark the publication of the Lectures in printed book form. The Trustees have also, from time to time, provided financial support for a variety of projects which, in various ways, have disseminated knowledge or have promoted to a wider public understanding of the law.

This, the 60th series of Lectures, was delivered by Professor Dame Hazel Genn at University College London and the University of Edinburgh. The Board of Trustees would like to record its appreciation to Professor Genn and also the two university law schools, which generously hosted these Lectures.

January 2008

KIM ECONOMIDES
Chairman of the Trustees

xiii

ACKNOWLEDGEMENTS

When Kim Economides, Chair of the Hamlyn Trustees, invited me to deliver the 2008 Hamlyn Lectures, I was honoured and daunted by the challenge of following such a distinguished list of predecessors. I am therefore very grateful to Kim for his support during the process of preparing the lectures. I am also grateful to Nicola Lacey, the 2007 Hamlyn Lecturer, for her encouragement and reassurance during the planning phase and to Sir Stephen Sedley for his advice. The first and last lectures were given at UCL and the second at Edinburgh University. I would like to thank Lady Hale for chairing the first lecture and Lord Clarke for chairing the final lecture. I am grateful to Professor Malcolm Grant, President and Provost of UCL, for making the time to preside over the final lecture, for his warm support throughout and for hosting the excellent final dinner. I am enormously indebted to Lisa Penfold of the Faculty of Laws at UCL for masterminding all of the invitations, replies, room bookings, receptions, menus and the thousand other things that needed to be done to ensure that everything ran smoothly. Lisa's quiet and calm efficiency was always reassuring, and her kindness hugely appreciated. Professor Sir Timothy O'Shea, Principal of Edinburgh University, graciously chaired the second lecture and hosted an excellent and enjoyable dinner. I would also like to thank Professor Douglas Brodie and Alison Stirling of Edinburgh Law School for taking charge of arrangements there and for organizing the lecture in the beautiful Playfair Library.

I took over as Dean of the UCL Law Faculty a couple of months before the lectures and could not have completed the writing without the support and encouragement of my Dean's Team, in particular John Lowry, Joanne Scott and Andrew Lewis. I also had valuable help from Rob Williams and Marc Mason. Edie Browne at Hong Kong University provided me with equipment, support and much printing out of articles and I am grateful to her and to Pauline Tang for being so accommodating. Neil Andrews kindly sent me material and I benefited from comments on the book manuscript from Judith Resnik, Peter Graham Harris, Lord Woolf and Tony Allen. In June 2009 a seminar was held at UCL to discuss the issues raised in the lectures with a distinguished panel comprising: Lord Woolf, Professor Michael Zander, Tony Allen, Professor Richard Moorhead and Professor Judith Resnik. I am grateful to the panellists for taking the time to offer their own perspectives on the lectures.

Finally, I want to pay tribute to Bea and Matt Appleby for instilling a sense of proportion at demanding times and to my husband Daniel Appleby for his rock-like support and willingness, as ever, to read and comment on drafts in the middle of the night.

August 2009

HAZEL GENN
University College London

1

Introduction: what is civil justice for?

Every civilised system of government requires that the
state should make available to all its citizens a means for
the just and peaceful settlement of disputes between them
as to their respective legal rights. The means provided are
courts of justice to which every citizen has a constitutional
right of access. Lord Diplock in *Bremer Vulkan Schiffbau
and Maschinenfabrik v South India Shipping Corp.* [1981]
AC 909, HL, p. 976.

The justification of a legal system and procedures must
be one of lesser evils, that legal resolution of disputes is
preferable to blood feuds, rampant crime and violence.
M. Bayles, 'Principles for legal procedure', *Law and
Philosophy*, 5:1 (1986), 33–57, 57.

The first impulse of a rudimentary soul is to do justice by
his own hand. Only at the cost of mighty historical efforts
has it been possible to supplant in the human soul the idea
of self-obtained justice by the idea of justice entrusted to
authorities. Eduardo J. Couture, 'The nature of the judicial
process', *Tulane Law Review*, 25 (1950), 1–28, 7.

The last fifteen years has been a period of significant change
within civil justice systems around the globe and the fundamental reform of English civil justice which was part of
that movement is now a decade old. This therefore seems an
opportune moment for reflection. In choosing civil justice as

my topic for the Hamlyn Lectures 2008, I am straying into territory well marked out by experts such as Sir Jack Jacob, Michael Zander, J.A. Jolowicz, Adrian Zuckerman and, of course, in his own time, Jeremy Bentham. But my ambition in these lectures is to offer a somewhat different perspective on civil justice. I am interested in theoretical questions about the social purpose and function of civil justice (in particular in common law systems) and empirical questions about how the civil justice system works in light of those purposes. My perspective on civil justice is shaped by the experience of nearly three decades spent studying how the civil justice system operates in practice. I have sat in people's homes talking about civil justice problems and why they do or don't want to litigate or wish they had or hadn't. I have sat in waiting rooms and at the backs of courts and tribunals talking to litigants before and after their hearings. I have sat in court offices with listing clerks trying to extract information from antiquated computer systems that still glow green. I have ploughed through muddled court files. I have talked to solicitors and barristers and judges and I have watched the professionals at work. My approach is thereby grounded in an empirical understanding of what the English civil justice system does, how it operates and how its work relates to the expectations and needs of the 'common people'.[1]

In his Hamlyn Lectures on civil justice in 1987, Sir Jack Jacob remarked that 'the system of civil justice is of transcendent importance for the people of this country, just as

---

[1] This phrase is used in describing the objectives of the Hamlyn Lectures as specified in the terms of trust in 1948, see http://law.exeter.ac.uk/ hamlyn/documents/hamlyntrustorder.pdf

it is for the people of every country.[2] He defined the civil justice system as the substantive law, machinery and procedures for vindicating and defending civil claims – in effect, the entire system of the administration of justice in civil matters. Adopting this broad definition, my starting point is that the machinery of civil justice sustains social stability and economic growth by providing public processes for peacefully resolving civil disputes, for enforcing legal rights and for protecting private and personal rights.[3] The civil justice system provides the legal architecture for the economy to operate effectively, for agreements to be honoured and for the power of government to be scrutinised and limited. The civil law maps out the boundaries of social and economic behaviour, while the civil courts resolve disputes when they arise. In this way, the civil courts publicly reaffirm norms and behavioural standards for private citizens, businesses and public bodies. Bargains between strangers are possible because rights and responsibilities are determined by a settled legal framework and are enforceable by the courts if promises are not kept. Under the rule of law, government is accountable for its actions and will be checked if it exceeds its powers. The courts are not the only vehicle for sending these messages, but they contribute quietly and significantly to social and economic well-being. They play a part in the sense that we live in an orderly society where there are rights and protections, and that these rights and protections can be made good.

---

[2] Sir Jack Jacob, *The Fabric of English Civil Justice* (Sweet & Maxwell, 1987), p. 1.

[3] For a helpful contemporary formulation see Australian Government Productivity Commission, *Report on Government Services 2008*, vol. 1, Part C 'Justice', Preface.

If the law is the skeleton that supports liberal democracies,[4] then the machinery of civil justice is some of the muscle and ligaments that make the skeleton work.

My objective in this book is to raise some questions about modern trends in civil justice policy in England and around the world, in the context of my own very settled views about the social importance of a well-functioning civil justice system. In particular, I want to focus on the decline of civil justice – the downgrading of the importance of civil justice, the degradation of civil court facilities and the diversion of civil cases to private dispute resolution, accompanied by an anti-litigation/anti-adjudication rhetoric that interprets these developments as socially positive.

Before starting, however, it is necessary to clear some conceptual undergrowth. The fact that Sir Jack, in his 1987 lectures, rather side-stepped the opportunity to say more about the social significance of civil justice might not have been accidental. One of the problems in discussing the social purpose of civil justice is the obstacle of terminology and definition. Or perhaps it really involves quite deep questions about how we conceptualise the civil justice system and whether it is a *system* in any sense.

When I mentioned to colleagues that I was giving the Hamlyn Lectures, after a sharp intake of breath the immediate response was generally 'What are they on?' After replying with the broad title of 'civil justice', most people would nod and mutter something like 'Oh that's nice'. But

---

[4] Metaphor borrowed from B. Tamanaha, *On The Rule of Law: History, Politics, Theory* (Cambridge University Press, 2004), 'Law is the skeleton that holds the liberal system upright and gives it form and stability', p. 36.

a few of my more penetrating critics would ask, 'What do you mean by civil justice?' As I reflected more deeply on the answer to that question and considered literature from around the world on civil justice reform, the purpose of civil justice, adjudication, vanishing trials, settlement and alternative dispute resolution (ADR) – all of which are discussed in this book – I became increasingly aware that issues I have touched on in the past are perhaps even more complicated than I had appreciated.

The shape of civil justice

The work of the civil courts reflects the cumulative choices of citizens and business about whether, when, how and how far to press and defend civil suits. There are many stakeholders in the civil justice system and a wide variety of civil justice problems. One of the difficulties of conceptualising civil justice as compared with criminal justice is its sheer complexity. The civil justice 'system' is arguably more varied and complex than the criminal justice system. In criminal justice it is possible to trace a consistent and relatively limited range of processes and decision-making bodies that inexorably leads towards a prosecution, normally involving the State as the prosecutor and an individual accused as the defendant. By contrast with criminal justice, civil cases involve a wide range of potential claimants and defendants with many different party configurations. In civil cases, claimants mobilise the legal system as a matter of choice and generally when other attempts to settle their dispute with a defendant have failed.

5

I wrote in my UCL Inaugural Lecture on civil justice more than a decade ago[5] that one of the problems in understanding civil justice is its complexity in terms of range of subject matter and configurations of parties and that this diversity inhibits conceptualisation and theoretical development – so many different types of parties, so many different types of dispute. We know from studies of legal problems around the world during the last decade[6] that potentially justiciable civil disputes involving private citizens represent the stuff and difficulties of everyday life: disputes with neighbours over behaviour or land; problems with landlords; money problems; employment problems; arguments over faulty goods and poor services; claims against insurance companies; social landlords seeking to evict indigent tenants. This variety of rights claims, grievances and quarrels leads to the difficulty of generalising about 'civil problems'. Within what we think of as the civil

---

[5] H. Genn, 'Understanding civil justice' in M. Freeman (ed.), *Law and Public Opinion in the 20th Century*, Current Legal Problems vol. 50 (Oxford University Press, 1997), pp. 155–87.

[6] H. Genn, *Paths to Justice: What People Think and Do About Going to Law* (Hart, 1999); P. Pleasence, A. Buck, N. Balmer, H. Genn, A. O'Grady and M. Smith, *Causes of Action: Civil Law and Social Justice* (The Stationery Office, 2004). Other examples include: *Consultancy Study on the Demand for and Supply of Legal and Related Services* (Hong Kong Department of Justice, 2008); C. Coumarelos, Z. Wei and A. Zhou, *Justice Made to Measure: NSW legal needs survey in disadvantaged areas* (Law and Justice Foundation of New South Wales, 2006); M. Murayama, 'Experiences of problems and disputing behaviour in Japan', *Meiji Law Journal*, 14 (2007), 1–59; B.C.J. Van Velthoven and M.J. ter Voert, *Geschilbeslechtingsdelta 2003* (WODC, 2004); M. Gramatikov, 'Multiple justiciable problems in Bulgaria' (Tilburg University Legal Studies Working Paper No. 16/2008, 2008).

justice system, individual citizens may bring actions against other individuals, or against large companies, or against public bodies. Financial institutions and public authorities regularly pursue actions against individual citizens. The dynamics of dispute resolution vary significantly in relation to the distribution of power and resources within litigation. Who can most easily afford the cost of pursuing or defending? Who can most easily afford to wait for a resolution? What an individual claimant suing an insurance company might want from the civil justice system is likely to look very different from what a social tenant seeking to resist possession from his landlord might want.[7]

Economic activity is facilitated by a complex system of legally enforceable rights and obligations, and corporate bodies make heavy use of the civil courts. In the sphere of business disputes there is a wide range of matters over which companies may argue and, again, considerable variation in the configuration of disputing parties: small companies suing each other; large companies suing each other; large companies suing small enterprises and vice versa. In common with disputes involving private citizens, the dynamics of commercial disputes are influenced by the distribution of power and resources.

But the analytical problem is more complicated than simply recognising the variety of disputes with their diverse dynamics. Sir Jack Jacob argued that the term 'civil justice' describes the entire system of the administration of justice in civil matters. In his view, the ambit of civil justice 'is wide and

---

[7] For a discussion of this variety see H. Genn, *Solving Civil Justice Problems: What might be best?*, Scottish Consumer Council Seminar on Civil Justice, 19 January 2005, www.ucl.ac.uk/laws/academics/profiles/docs/genn_05_civil_justice_problems.pdf

far-reaching and its bounds have not yet been fully chartered; it encompasses the whole area of what is comprised in civil procedural law'.[8] Michael Zander, in his Hamlyn Lectures in 1999, adopted a similar approach by arguing that 'civil justice concerns the handling of disputes between citizens arising out of civil as opposed to criminal, law. The phrase is normally used to signify all stages of civil disputes by courts, including the issue of proceedings, settlement, trial and post-trial appeals'.[9] But in drawing civil justice so widely, these definitions bring together disputes between citizens, disputes between business and other corporate bodies, and also family disputes. More importantly, they draw in conflicts between citizens and public bodies including central government agencies. Sometimes when people speak of civil justice they are thinking of it as somewhat separate from family and administrative justice. On other occasions they are referring to civil justice as everything that isn't criminal. It is important to be clear because there are conceptual, constitutional and practical differences between disputes involving the individual and the state, disputes following family breakdown, and civil and commercial disputes. The distinctions matter because there are different views about the theoretical purpose of the role of the public courts within those sub-fields or divisions of civil justice and because, to some extent, there are variations in justice policy in relation to those sub-divisions.

When we consider personal injury litigation, consumer disputes or debt cases we are dealing with dissimilar subject matter but within a common framework – that of disputes about

[8] Jacob, *The Fabric of English Civil Justice*, p. 2.
[9] M. Zander, *The State of Justice*, 51st Hamlyn Lectures (Sweet & Maxwell, 2000), p. 27.

compensation for injuries, breach of contract, negligent performance of obligations, etc. In each of these cases the dispute will come to court as a result of a difference of view about a factual situation where the law and the courts offer a remedy. The difference of view cannot be resolved between the parties. If it could, it would not be a dispute. In most cases the claimant wants money to compensate for their loss. The defendant will not or cannot pay the compensation. Will not – because he genuinely believes he has done nothing wrong – or cannot because he is impecunious. The coercive power of the court is mobilised by the claimant in order to achieve what he or she believes is a right and which the claimant has been unable to achieve by force of negotiation and argument. The action of bringing suit in the courts confirms the belief of the claimant in his right to a remedy and underlines the social function of the court in that it is prepared to hear and decide the claim on behalf of the claimant.

When we consider relationship breakdown and contact with children, we are once more thinking about disputes, but outside of the realm of contract or tort and instead in the context of the pain of family conflict. Again there are differences of view about factual situations. What is a fair division of family property? Who is best placed to care for the children?

However, when we speak about judicial review of decisions by government, we are in rather different territory. Here the role of the courts is less about dispute resolution and the promulgation of norms and standards in relation to the behaviour of citizens or in the conduct of business, and more about the exercise of a constitutional responsibility to ensure that the executive governs according to law. In effect, these cases are about the rule of law in action.

One of the questions raised in this book is what importance we should attach to judicial determination in civil justice as compared with private settlement. But it is evident that ideas about the importance of adjudication and the role of the judiciary will differ depending not only on the position of the judge in the hierarchy of English courts and tribunals but also on whether the judge is being called upon to adjudicate in disputes between citizens, between family members, between businesses, or between a government and its citizens. Because all of these justiciable matters are swept up together in the administration of civil justice, it is difficult when considering influences on government civil justice policy to limit discussion to one particular sub-division of civil justice. Thus, although much of my focus in this book is on the role of the courts in non-family civil disputes, rather than family or administrative justice, I want to make clear that the developments I trace in civil justice discourse and policy are both influenced by and will have an impact on the work of the courts in relation to family and administrative justice.

What is the civil justice *system*?

The definitions of civil justice offered by Sir Jack Jacob and Michael Zander include not only the substantive law affecting civil rights and duties but the machinery provided by the state and the judiciary for the resolution of civil justice disputes and grievances. The administration of civil justice includes the institutional architecture, the procedures and apparatus for processing and adjudicating civil claims and disputes. The system – if it is a system – is crafted partly by the government through the provision of buildings, resources, personnel, judiciary and fees for suit, and partly by the judiciary who are the guardians of procedure. The judiciary are responsible for practice statements, guidance and rule changes and in many common law jurisdictions have had a strong influence in reviews and reforms of civil justice.

The civil justice *system* is partly about substantive rights,[10] but perhaps more importantly it is about the provision that society makes for citizens and business to bring civil suits – the *right of action* and the *machinery to make good* that right. A critical question for those interested in civil justice is not 'what rights do we give?', but having given those rights, having imposed duties and obligations, having devised a policy for enforcing behaviour or ameliorating some social ill, what opportunities and structures do we provide for the public to enforce those rights and obligations or make good their entitlements?

This then raises the question of whether the law, structures and processes for pursuing and resolving claims constitute a 'system'. The concept of a system suggests a group of interacting, interrelated or interdependent elements forming a complex whole or a functionally related group of elements. To that extent, the machinery of civil justice does, indeed, represent a system in that elements are interrelated and interact and that disturbance in one part of the system will produce predictable and sometimes unpredictable consequences for other parts of the system. Unfortunately, although civil justice is referred to as a system, policy initiatives have not always well understood the nature of the interrelationships and interactions or taken them into account.

---

[10] See the discussion by J.A. Jolowicz in 'On the nature and purpose of civil procedural law', Chapter 3 in J.A. Jolowicz, *On Civil Procedure* (Cambridge University Press, 2000).

Indeed, it is arguable that recent policies in some areas have been almost calculated to cause disturbance and dysfunctional ripples elsewhere. The introduction of conditional fee arrangements ('CFA')[11] – a measure to meet the access needs of middle-income earners – has created complex incentives and disincentives around the cost of actions and pressures to settle. The financing of the civil courts has, in the past, incorporated cross-subsidies. Thus the fees paid by institutional claimants in thousands of undefended debt cases provide a solid cushion of support for the activities of other parts of the civil justice system. As a result, policies for *reducing* the number of cases issued in court in certain categories may impact work in other areas and inevitably lead to a loss of income for the civil justice system as a whole.

The significance of procedure

The civil justice 'system' then comprises the substantive law, the civil procedure rules, courts and the judiciary. Although I do not want to focus on the detail of civil procedure, it is necessary to think about the purpose of civil procedural rules, since it is these rules that have been the main target of civil justice reformers. There seems to be common

---

[11] A form of 'no win, no fee' arrangement between lawyer and client. Originally introduced by S58 of the Courts and Legal Services Act 1990, such arrangements allow solicitors to charge clients involved in civil disputes a success fee ('uplift') if the client wins at trial or settles with the defendant. If the case is lost, the client is not liable for the solicitor's fee and an insurance premium covers liability for the opponent's legal costs. Although initially limited to personal injury litigation, insolvency and human rights cases in the 1990 Act, the Access to Justice Act 1999 extended CFAs to all civil claims with the exception of family cases.

agreement around the world that a critical challenge in solving the problems of cost, complexity and delay in civil justice is that of getting the rules right. But why are the procedural rules so important? The answer is that the rules guarantee procedural fairness, and procedural fairness is important both in its own right and through its link with substantive justice.

It has been argued that legal procedure is 'a ritual of extreme social significance' and that the characteristics of 'a civilized country' are revealed not so much through the substantive law as in the practice and procedure of the courts.[12] Jeremy Bentham saw the rules of procedure as being central to the machinery of civil justice. For Bentham, the power of procedure was in the link between evidence and correct decisions (rectitude) and the role of procedure in achieving accuracy in decision making continues to be seen as central today by procedural scholars.[13] The system of procedure is designed to ensure that judges have all of the appropriate evidence available so that they can find the material facts and apply the substantive law to those facts. In this way, procedural rules reflect a sense of justice. Procedure is the means by which substantive rights are enforced.

---

[12] C.J. Hamson, 'In court in two countries: civil procedure in England and France', *Times* (London), 15 November 1949, quoted in Margaret Y.K. Woo and Y. Wang, 'Civil justice in China: an empirical study of courts in three provinces', *American Journal of Comparative Law*, 53 (2005), 911.

[13] A.A.S. Zuckerman, 'Justice in crisis: comparative aspects of civil procedure' in A.A.S. Zuckerman (ed.), *Civil Justice in Crisis: Comparative Perspectives of Civil Procedure* (Oxford University Press, 1999).

Indeed, it has recently been argued that rather than being *mere* rules, the procedures devised for adjudicating civil cases are essentially 'the means by which society expresses its underlying meaning'.[14] Procedure is important because of its link to substantive outcome. If substantive justice lies in the correct application of legal principles to a factual situation, then procedures that increase the likelihood of a correct decision being reached are vital.

It is also argued that procedure is important to litigants. There is a relatively substantial body of literature in social psychology that provides firm empirical evidence first, that those involved in legal decision-making processes are able to distinguish procedure from outcome and second, that fair procedures make losing more acceptable and contribute to the legitimacy of the decision-making body.[15] According to this research, the critical elements that contribute to perceptions of fairness are the opportunity to be heard, the opportunity to influence the decision maker, even-handedness of the decision maker, and being treated with courtesy and respect. Thus procedural justice is not only theoretically important as the route to substantively correct decision making but is an important influence on user perceptions of the fairness of legal processes. In considering the significance of procedural justice, Lawrence Solum argues that it is fundamentally about participation:

[14] J.M. Jacob, *Civil Justice in the Age of Human Rights* (Ashgate, 2007), p. 3.
[15] E.A. Lind and T.R. Tyler, *The Social Psychology of Procedural Justice* (Plenum, 1988); S. Blader and T.R. Tyler, 'A four component model of procedural justice: Defining the meaning of a "fair" process', *Personality and Social Psychology Bulletin*, 29 (2003), 747–58.

> Procedural justice is deeply entwined with the old and
> powerful idea that a process that guarantees rights of
> meaningful participation is an essential prerequisite for
> the legitimate authority of action-guiding legal norms.[16]

Solum further suggests that while meaningful participation in
legal proceedings requires parties to have notice of the case
against them and the opportunity to be heard, it also requires
a reasonable balance between cost and accuracy. However, the
challenge facing any civil justice system is where to find the
balance between efficiency and substantive justice. How much
justice can we afford? Or, as I argue in the next chapter, perhaps it is more a question of how much justice can we afford to
forego? How much procedural justice do you need to achieve
an appropriate degree of substantive justice? Even in the early
part of the nineteenth century, Bentham was concerned about
the burden on both parties involved in litigation.[17] He argued
that it was important to reduce the delays, vexations and
expenses involved in pursuing civil litigation. In Bentham's
terminology 'vexation' is an amalgam of the frustrations, dis-
tresses and irritations involved in pursuing legal action. The
challenge, then, is to find the balance between procedures
that are seen as fair, that contribute to substantive justice and
that provide reasonable access to justice so that rights can be
enforced, but are not so complicated or expensive as to make
proceedings inaccessible. But what is the correct measure of

---

[16] L.B. Solum, 'Procedural Justice', *Southern California Law Review*, 78
(2004) 181.
[17] A.J. Draper, 'Corruptions in the administration of justice: Bentham's
critique of civil procedure, 1806–1811', *Journal of Bentham Studies*, 7
(2004).

procedure? Litigant satisfaction with process and outcome? Correct decisions and substantive justice? How accurate do we need to be? When we say the outcome was 'correct', what does that mean? Adrian Zuckerman has argued that in the end, measuring the success of procedures in doing justice is a complex judgement relating to rectitude of decision, time and cost. 'There is no perfect rectitude of decision, justice cannot be dispensed instantly without some delay, and justice cannot be absolutely free of cost constraints. Each system has had to balance the competing demands and strike a compromise.'[18]

Civil justice as a public good

Civil justice serves a number of purposes. Essentially, the civil justice system provides the legal structure for the economy to operate effectively and for the power of government to be scrutinised and limited. It serves a private function in providing peaceful, authoritative and coercive termination of disputes between citizens, companies and public bodies. Those are its dispute-resolution and behaviour-modification functions.[19] As usual, Sir Jack Jacob manages to convey economically most of the private functions of civil justice as follows: '[Civil justice] plays a role of crucial importance in the life and culture of a civilised community. It constitutes the machinery for obtaining what Lord Brougham called "justice between man and man." It manifests the political will of the State that civil remedies be provided for civil rights and claims,

[18] Zuckerman, *Civil Justice in Crisis*, p. 11.
[19] M. Bayles, 'Principles for legal procedure', *Law and Philosophy*, 5:1 (1986), 33–57, 57.

and that civil wrongs, whether they consist of infringements of private rights in the enjoyment of life, liberty, property or otherwise, be made good, so far as practicable, by compensation and satisfaction, or restrained, if necessary, by appropriate relief.'[20]

But civil justice has important and extensive social functions that go beyond settling disputes between 'man and man' and to this extent must be regarded as a public rather than a private benefit. It has functions in relation to social justice, economic stability and social order. The law both reflects and promotes social change. Civil justice is the means by which citizens are able to uphold their substantive civil rights against other citizens. It provides a framework in which business can be done and investment can be protected, thus supporting economic activity and development. Lord Woolf has argued that civil justice 'safeguards the rights of individuals, regulates their dealings with others and enforces the duties of government'.[21] Lord Bingham has argued that, in enabling citizens to assert their substantive civil rights against the state itself, the civil justice system plays a 'truly essential role' in furthering the rule of law.[22] The head of civil justice, Sir Anthony Clarke MR, has argued that

[20] Sir Jack Jacob, 'The reform of civil procedural law', reprinted in *The Reform of Civil Procedural Law and Other Essays in Civil Procedure* (Sweet & Maxwell, 1982), p. 1.

[21] The Rt Hon. Lord Woolf, *Access to Justice: Interim Report to the Lord Chancellor on the Civil Justice System in England and Wales* (HMSO, 1995), Chapter 1, para. 1.

[22] Lord Bingham, 'The Rule of Law', Sixth David Williams Annual Lecture, Centre for Public Law, Cambridge University, http://www.cpl.law.cam. ac.uk/past_activities/

without an effective civil justice system, substantive civil laws are no more than words and that the rule of law becomes an 'aspiration' rather than a reality. The civil justice system must therefore be 'readily accessible and effective'.[23] He has also made clear that although criminal justice 'undoubtedly has a higher profile in the UK', an effective civil justice system is an essential aspect of our commitment to the rule of law.[24]

Thus within a common law system, the purpose of the civil courts goes beyond dispute resolution. Jolowicz contends that the broad social goals of civil justice are to demonstrate the effectiveness of the law and to allow judges to perform their function of clarifying, developing and applying the law.[25] In determining the merits in individual disputes, the judiciary are publicly stating the law, reinforcing norms of social and economic behaviour, identifying the limits of executive power and publicising the values of the society. Courts make authoritative declarations of what the law is, which obligations must be performed and which responsibilities must be discharged. In effect, the courts reflect, communicate and reinforce society's dominant social and economic values. To this extent the law

[23] Sir Anthony Clarke, 'The importance of civil justice: nationally and internationally', American Bar Association Conference, London, 3 October 2007, para. 9, www.judiciary.gov.uk/docs/speeches/mr_ american_bar_assoc_031007.pdf

[24] Sir Anthony Clarke, 'A UK perspective on EU civil justice – impact on domestic dispute resolution', EU Civil Justice Day Conference, The Law Society, London, October 2007, para. 3, www.judiciary.gov.uk/docs/ speeches/mr_ukeu_civiljustice_251007.pdf

[25] Jolowicz, *On Civil Procedure*, p. 71.

is a statement of values.[26] In a common law system (even one with significant statutory law) these ends are achieved by the promulgation and development of the common law. That promulgation comes through published decisions. As Roy Goode noted in his Hamlyn Lectures on Commercial Law, most of commercial law is found in jurisprudence rather than statute, reflecting the sense that for commercial activity to flourish, the legal system that accommodates it must be 'flexible and responsive to rapid change'. The role of the courts is to 'respect and enforce reasonable mercantile practice while refusing recognition to agreements offensive to public policy'.[27]

The social importance of the justice system is reflected by its significance in literature. Civil justice texts are replete with quotes from Bentham, Shakespeare, Dickens and Kafka. The permeation of justice and justice system issues throughout literature could be a manifestation of Jacob's 'transcendent' importance of civil justice. The significance of the civil justice system is also reflected in the majesty of court buildings – in the iconography of justice.[28] But the question is, important in what way? Does the civil justice system have practical significance to the everyday resolution of trouble and disputes? Is it of significance because it offers the ultimate backstop providing a sense of order and security? The answer is that it

---

[26] O.M. Fiss, 'Against settlement', *Yale Law Journal*, 93 (1984), 1073–90; Marc Galanter, 'The radiating effects of courts' in K. Boyum and L. Mather (eds), *Empirical Theories About Courts*, (Longman, 1983), p. 117.

[27] R. Goode, *Commercial Law in the Next Millennium*, 49th Hamlyn Lectures (Sweet & Maxwell, 1998), p. 10.

[28] See J. Resnik, 'Courts: in and out of sight, site and cite', *Villanova Law Review*, 53 (2008), 101–38.

is of significance because the law fixes obligations and duties through rules governing social and economic and governmental behaviour. It is of significance because it is in the light of those rules that people arrange their affairs and seek to avoid disputes. The significance lies in the individual decisions affecting the lives of private citizens, businesses and public bodies and, more importantly in social terms, in the authoritative rulings of the judiciary together with their articulation of their reasoning and the principles applied.

The importance of adjudication

> The trial is a site of deep accountability where facts are exposed and responsibility assessed. A place where the ordinary politics of personal interaction are suspended, the fictions that shield us from embarrassment and moral judgment are stripped away.[29]

While the private value of civil justice is in the termination of disputes – whether by negotiation, solicitor-generated settlements or facilitated settlement through ADR or judicial settlement or judicial determination – the *public* function of civil justice is, in this way, explicitly or implicitly linked with assumptions about the value of *adjudication*. The public value of civil justice is in reinforcing values and practices. It comes from authoritative statements of what the law is, who has rights and how those rights are to be vindicated. 'The norms and behaviours contained within the law become internalised

---

[29] M. Galanter, 'A world without trials', *Journal of Dispute Resolution*, 7 (2006), 7–34, 22.

and underpin the actions of members of the community in their daily interactions.'[30] This is the 'shadow' cast by the law – in effect its public value.

It is arguable that for civil justice to perform its public role – to cast its shadow – adjudication and public promulgation of decisions are critical. This is the public role of the judge. Adjudication provides the framework for settlements – the shadow in which settlements can be reached. That it is underpinned by coercive power provides the background threat that brings unwilling litigants to the negotiating table. While the reality is that most cases settle, a flow of adjudicated cases is necessary to provide guidance on the law and, most importantly, to create the credible threat of litigation if settlement is not achieved. Of course, the cases that are litigated are a peculiar subset of the dispute pyramid. They are the cases that could not be settled either because the facts were not clear or because they raised original problems or because one side was too intransigent to settle or, perhaps, because the costs were too high to settle. It is therefore a matter of chance which cases proceed to litigation. But those cases that do proceed to litigation provide the material for the elaboration of the common law and provide a useful social function in giving the courts the opportunity to restate or develop the law. What arrives at the court is to some extent a reflection of access to justice or the resources of the parties to proceed as far as adjudication and, indeed, appeal. Those cases that reach appeal reflect patterns of access to the courts.

[30] M. Galanter, 'The radiating effects of courts', ibid; Department of Justice, Victoria, Australia, *Justice Statement* – Chapter 2.0, 'Justice and the need for change' (2004), para. 2.3.1.

Take the case of Mrs Donoghue and the snail in the ginger beer bottle, decided by the House of Lords in 1932.[31] The case effectively transformed the law. Whatever view is taken of the decision, the case established protection for consumers, created an incentive for those who create risks to take care and the possibility of redress for those harmed by negligent actions. In this way the common law has developed on the back of private and business disputes and thousands of cases have been settled in its wake. The access to justice implications of *Donoghue v Stevenson* and the question of whether such a case would be likely to reach the courts today are considered in the next chapter.

In these expressions of civil justice as a public good we find a number of interrelated issues that are addressed in this book: the public value of the civil justice system as the rule of law in operation; the role of procedures in ensuring fairness in the operation of the system; and the significance of adjudication as the public expression of norms and values and authoritative declaration of the law. All of these linked elements are currently under what might be seen as re-evaluation or threat – depending on one's perspective. The system as a whole is threatened by resource constraints; procedural rules that express social values about on what evidence liability can be fixed are questioned as being too elaborate and only serving the interests of lawyers; and adjudication is regarded as unnecessary and unpleasant. But these are important issues. Resnik has argued that adjudication is about more than an

---

[31] *Donoghue (or McAlister) v Stevenson* [1932] All ER Rep 1; [1932] AC 562; House of Lords.

opportunity to debate conflicting rights claims. That it is itself a democracy-enhancing practice:

> [A]djudication sits as a democratic practice because within its parameters, it can reconfigure authority, including subjecting the state itself to disgorge information and provide remedies.[32]

Recently both Adrian Zuckerman[33] and David Luban have separately argued that adjudication is a public good and something more than a public service. As Luban writes:

> Instead of treating adjudication as a social service that the state provides disputing parties to keep the peace, the public life conception treats disputing parties as … an occasion for the law to work itself pure … the litigants serve as nerve endings registering the aches and pains of the body politic, which the court attempts to treat by refining the law. Using litigants as stimuli for refining the law is a legitimate public interest in the literal sense … The law is a self-portrait of our politics, and adjudication is at once the interpretation and the refinement of the portrait.[34]

However, the idea that the civil justice system is both a private and a public good implies that the public are able to access the machinery for enforcing their rights and that the

---

[32] J. Resnik and D. Curtis, 'Representing justice: from Renaissance iconography to twenty-first century courthouses', Proceedings of the American Philosophical Society, 151 (2007), 139.

[33] Zuckerman, *Civil Justice in Crisis*, p. 10.

[34] D. Luban, 'Settlements and the erosion of the public realm', *Georgetown Law Journal*, 83 (1995), 2638.

procedures for enforcement are fair.[35] The issue of what kind of access to justice is offered by the civil justice system in practice is addressed in the next chapter.

Threats to civil justice

A fundamental argument that runs through this book is that recent policy on the administration of civil justice has disregarded the social importance of a well-functioning civil justice system, that both external and internal pressures threaten the future of civil justice and that these threats are visible in jurisdictions around the globe.

The *external threat* to civil justice arises from the unstoppable burgeoning of criminal justice in an environment of resource constraints. The increasing regulation and criminalisation of social and economic activity, the process demands of human rights legislation and the associated costs of incarceration have led to a substantial increase in the amount of public money devoted to criminal justice. In England, the recent creation of the Ministry of Justice means that the administration of civil and criminal justice, the personnel and activities of courts and tribunals, as well as the functioning of the growing penal system have been melded into a single government department. It is arguable that with a single justice budget, the urgent and politically charged resource pressure of criminal justice has led to a climate in which the importance of civil justice has become obscured and the functioning of

---

[35] R.L. Sandefur, 'Access to civil justice and race, class, and gender inequality', *Annual Review of Sociology*, 34 (2008), 339–58.

civil justice has been downgraded. In this respect, this book follows neatly from a central theme of the previous Hamlyn Lectures given by Nicola Lacey – namely the increasing politicisation of criminal justice during the past three decades, the scale and intensity of criminalisation and the increasing focus on criminal justice as an indicator of the competence of successive governments.[36]

Concurrent with this external threat there is an *internal threat* to civil justice emanating from sections of the judiciary, legal practice and the emerging alternative dispute resolution profession in search of a market for their services. In the process of seeking necessary and laudable improvements to the administration of civil justice, voluble reformers have attacked its principles and purpose in a 'postmodernist' rhetoric which undermines the value of legal determination, suggests that adjudication is always unpleasant and unnecessary, and finally promotes the conviction that there are no rights that cannot be compromised and that every conflict represents merely a clash of morally equivalent interests.

A powerful meeting of minds has developed between an emerging profession of private dispute resolvers and judicial opinion formers which perfectly suits the financial realities of a cash-strapped justice system struggling to process a growing number of criminal defendants. In this atmosphere, State responsibility for providing effective and peaceful forums for resolving civil disputes is being shrugged off through a discourse which locates civil justice as a private matter rather

---

[36] N. Lacey, *The Prisoners' Dilemma*, 59th Hamlyn Lectures (Cambridge University Press, 2008).

than a public and socially important good. The civil courts and judiciary may not be a public service like health or transport systems, but through the performance of this critical social and economic function, the judicial system services the public in a way that transcends private interests.

While proceduralists worry about detailed improvements to the civil procedure rules, I would suggest that the underpinning structures and processes of the civil justice system may be crumbling. It is therefore timely to take a look at civil justice, not by focusing on the stitches in the engrossing tapestry of procedural rules, but by standing back and looking at what has been happening to policy and practice in the context of a shared understanding about the purpose and value of civil justice in modern, democratic societies and, in particular, in the common law system in England.

2

Civil justice: how much is enough?

Having drawn attention to the social and economic importance of civil justice, this chapter considers the surprising coincidence during the past decade of worldwide 'crises' in civil justice. It examines the reform programmes put in place around the world – in response to these perceived crises and access to justice concerns – and discusses the interesting disconnection of these reviews and reforms from any empirical understanding about access to justice. The chapter concludes with a discussion of recent comparative evidence about the responsiveness of the civil justice system to the needs of the public and a reflection on the question of how much civil justice we need and how much we can afford to forego in light of the purposes of civil justice.

Civil justice in crisis around the world

If the significance of civil justice to governments around the world were to be judged merely by the number and tonnage of review reports, then clearly it is very significant indeed. The last decade has seen a global explosion of reviews, analyses and reforms of civil justice systems. Although the English civil justice system has been the subject of complaint and report at least since the middle of the nineteenth century, the fundamental review of English civil justice undertaken by Lord Woolf during 1994–6 has to be viewed in that wider

context. It was only one of a number of similar reviews and
reform programmes that started in California and Australia,
were repeated in several Australian states and then seemed to
spread around the world to New Zealand, several provinces in
Canada, Hong Kong and Scotland. All were apparently undertaken in response to existing or impending crises in civil justice. Indeed, a collection of scholarly papers published in 1999
edited by Adrian Zuckerman was dramatically entitled *Civil
Justice in Crisis*.[1] The collection dealt with trends and reforms
to civil justice around the world including Europe, the USA
and the Far East. The underpinning philosophy and reform
proposals of these reviews are discussed later in the chapter,
but first I want to consider the nature of the crisis that seemed
to be afflicting these very different jurisdictions and legal cultures at precisely the same time. What was it a crisis of and
whose crisis was it? Why did civil justice systems around the
world have to change at that particular moment? Of course
there are always adjustments and improvements that can be
made to any system and few would argue that there was no
scope for modernising English civil justice in the mid-1990s.
But what is intriguing is the *crisis* rhetoric and the sense of
urgency about change. And even more curious is the fact that
in many places the apparent crisis was occurring at a time of
declining pressure on the civil courts.

There are varying explanations for this extraordinary
worldwide coincidence of civil justice 'crises' and explosion of

[1] A.A.S. Zuckerman, 'Justice in crisis: comparative aspects of civil
procedure' in A.A.S. Zuckerman (ed.), *Civil Justice in Crisis: Comparative
Perspectives of Civil Procedure* (Oxford University Press, 1999).

civil justice reform programmes depending on whether the explanation is being provided by procedural scholars, political scientists, policy makers, or law-reform bodies. But a decade on, reading through the reviews in chronological order, what is striking is the mutual adoption, replication and reinforcement of vocabulary and rhetoric as well as the accepted diagnoses, solutions and reform measures from jurisdiction to jurisdiction, legal culture to legal culture. What is also interesting is the extent to which some of the reviews seem to assume that the need for the review was so self-evident that justification was unnecessary.

Too much law or not enough access?

How are we to understand the source of these civil justice crises which, I will argue, have led to a damaging change in public discourse about, and representation of, the civil justice system and the value of judicial determination? A plausible explanation emerges from modern interest in the phenomenon of the 'Vanishing Trial'. Law and society scholars in the USA have been much preoccupied with the nature of their own presumed 'crisis' in civil justice in the context of disappearing trials. Having noted and charted the decline of trials in the USA over a period of thirty years, Marc Galanter[2] argues that this decline is not an isolated incident, but is closely connected to changes in the US legal environment over the same period. Galanter suggests that the decline is

[2] M. Galanter, 'A world without trials', *Journal of Dispute Resolution*, 7 (2006), 7–34.

not a continuation of the slow and gradual tendency towards greater pre-trial settlement of civil disputes but is a sudden and precipitous 'vanishing' of trials from civil courts. He links the disappearance of the trial to the alleged 'crisis' in civil justice. The crisis rhetoric, he argues, is primarily a backlash response to fundamental developments in civil justice since the 1930s. Galanter argues that the roots of the decline in trials can be found, paradoxically, in the expansion of legal remedies and protections for ordinary citizens that took place from the 1930s to the 1970s, including the establishment of the welfare state and the enforcement of civil rights. This expansion in rights was accompanied by an opening up of access to the courts, so that by the mid-1960s the courts, legislature and lawyers had transformed the legal landscape and ordinary people were in a position to mount legal challenges to powerful businesses and public bodies.

In particular, in the US context, Galanter points to an enlargement of tort remedies and a proliferation of 'new rights, new players on the legal stage (as in the consumer, environmental and women's movements), and new formats for legal services such as legal services for the poor and public interest law firms'.[3] During the same period, law schools grew, attracting politically active students who saw law as a vehicle for realising their commitment to social justice and social reform.

Galanter argues that these changes, and the calls in the mid-20th century for more 'access to justice', provoked a profound reaction. He suggests that business, political and

[3] Ibid, 7–34, 19.

other elites adopted what he terms a 'jaundiced' view of the civil justice system, pointing to what was deemed to be a litigation explosion – and what in England has been referred to as 'the compensation culture'. The jaundiced view of civil justice conjures up images of 'opportunistic claimants, egged on by greedy lawyers, and enabled by activist judges[4] and biased juries that capriciously award immense sums against blameless businesses and governments'.[5] He goes on to argue that in the USA this reaction led to tort reforms designed to limit corporate responsibility, reduce remedies and make access to the courts more difficult. In the process of achieving these changes, American civil justice has been depicted as a pathological system, inflicting devastating damage on the nation's health care and economic well-being. Galanter argues that 'although the available evidence overwhelmingly refutes these assertions, this set of beliefs, supported by folk-lore and powerfully reinforced by media coverage, has become the conventional wisdom'.[6]

In Galanter's view, the political discourse about the law now incorporates a 'narrative of moral decline' in which the worthy law of the 'good old days' has been appropriated and corrupted by 'greedy lawyers and self-pitying claimants'.[7] As a result, he argues there has been a loss of public confidence in the government's

---

[4] There is a particular concern in the USA about overly 'activist' judges. It is a pejorative term describing judges who too readily overturn decisions of the executive, who are guided principally by their own policy preferences rather than by a proper attention to legal principle.

[5] Ibid, 20.

[6] Ibid, 20.

[7] Ibid, 20.

ability to promote and supply accessible justice; there has been a trend towards private dispute-resolution processes and a retreat from investment in the justice system as a public good. He says: 'From the mid-1970s, tort reform, ADR, and anti-lawyer-ism were in the ascendant … The most prominent critique of the law was no longer "not enough justice" but "too much law".' He argues that 'in the new discourse about law, we are constantly reminded of the costs of law and litigation, but curiously tend to be forgetful of their benefits. The costs, all too evident, are presented vividly, frequently with exaggeration. On the other hand, the benefits are easily taken for granted and receive at most a perfunctory acknowledgment.'[8] At the same time, the reaction of judges seems to have been a recasting of their role from authoritative determination to promoters of dispute resolution.

The anti-law story suggests that society is in the grip of a litigation explosion or compensation culture, and that the solution is to be found in cutting down court procedure, diverting cases away from courts and pushing disputes into private resolution. The message is that 'rights' conflicts ought to be reframed or reconceptualised as 'clashes of interests' which can be satisfactorily reformulated as 'problems' which can then be solved through mediation. Most importantly, the Vanishing Trials narrative suggests that, in the US at least, the antipathy to trials is not simply about expense or delay. It is also about an aversion to the determination of corporate accountability in public forums. We now seem to have a modern paradox in which there is a proliferation of law and regulation, accompanied by a reduction in adjudication.

[8] Ibid, 21.

Galanter argues that we are witnessing a continuing legalisation of society accompanied by the atrophy of a central and emblematic legal institution.

But how does this story fit with developments in England? Comparing Galanter's US trial data with that of the High Court and county courts in England and Wales, Herbert Kritzer concluded in 2004 that 'in England and Wales, there is a pattern of decline in civil cases, but no such pattern in criminal cases'. Kritzer assumed that much of the decline in trials in civil cases during the previous decade could be attributed to a combination of changes in procedural rules, jurisdictional changes and the likely impact of ADR – although he acknowledged that there was no clear way to distribute the drop in trials among these various explanations.[9]

Updating Kritzer's analysis using more recent evidence from judicial statistics, Figures 2.1–2.5 show the rates for the issue of proceedings in the Queens Bench Division (QBD) of the High Court and the county courts (where most civil and commercial disputes are dealt with). These demonstrate a very clear trend that fits in well with Galanter's growth of rights narrative. Looking at the period between 1938 and 1990, we see a steep increase in the number of cases being commenced both in the QBD and in the county courts. But in common with other jurisdictions around the world, since the mid-1990s England has witnessed a reduction in the number of cases coming to court for authoritative adjudication. This trend is most marked in the High Court, but it is also evident in the county courts.

[9] H.M. Kritzer, 'Disappearing trials? A comparative perspective', *Journal of Empirical Legal Studies*, 1:3 (2004), 735–54, 752.

33

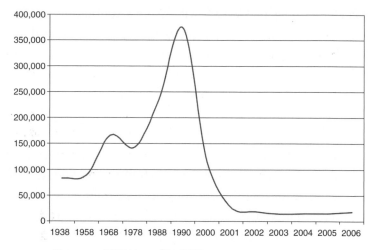

Figure 2.1 Writs issued in QBD

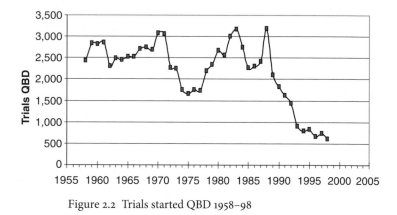

Figure 2.2 Trials started QBD 1958–98

County court claims show the same increasing trend, but then a decline after 1990, despite the change in jurisdiction between High Court and county courts introduced by the Courts and Legal Services Act 1990.

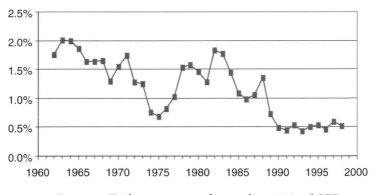

Figure 2.3 Trials as a per cent of proceedings initiated QBD

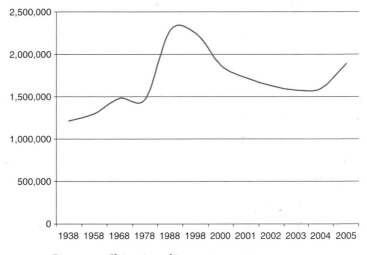

Figure 2.4 Claims issued in county court

Although in England there has always been a high rate of settlement in the 'shadow' of the law,[10] this trend has

---

[10] R.H. Mnookin and L. Kornhauser, 'Bargaining in the shadow of the law: The case of divorce', *Yale Law Journal*, 88 (1979), 950–97.

35

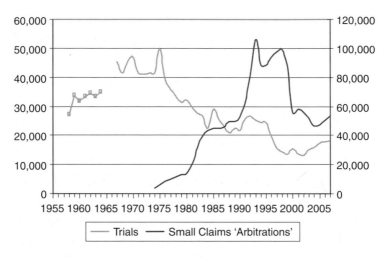

Figure 2.5 County court trials

accelerated over the last decade. While some of the factors identified in the USA may have been influencing these trends, Robert Dingwall has pointed out that in England this development has been a matter of deliberate government policy. He argues that:

> [S]uccessive UK governments have decided that, although civil justice may be a public service, it is not a public good in the sense that Lord Woolf asserted in his first report … they see the system as providing only private benefits for individuals rather than collective benefits for the society as a whole … The creation of precedents and the creation of law, through the civil justice system, is not perceived by government as contributing to the general welfare in the same way as state-provided education or health care.

Dingwall goes on to argue that unlike the situation in the USA, in England 'civil justice has always been a legitimate object of state policy'. [11]

This conclusion is supported by looking at the public service targets that the Lord Chancellor's Department, Department for Constitutional Affairs (DCA) and now the Ministry of Justice have set for themselves in recent years in which a reduction in the number of cases coming to the civil courts has been a target to be met and against which the success of the Department would be judged. Indeed, the precise opposite of the trend noted by Nicola Lacey in her Hamlyn Lectures in relation to criminal justice. Whether this is a matter for congratulation or concern depends to some extent on your perspective and your fundamental beliefs about the social function of civil justice and the development of common law. Not everyone sees the reduction in trials as a bad thing. Richard Susskind, for example, in his recent speculations on the future of law has predicted the end of lawyers and law as we know them and, without apparent anxiety, envisaged the prospect that, following the trend of banks, court buildings will become bars and restaurants. [12]

But why does the government want to see a reduction in the use of the civil courts at a time when law and regulation is proliferating and the government is explicitly increasing the number of people brought to the criminal courts? Is it because they believe that the civil courts are bad for the

---

[11] R. Dingwall and E. Cloatre, 'Vanishing trials?: An English perspective', *Journal of Dispute Resolution*, 7 (2006), 51–70, 67.

[12] R. Susskind, *The End of Lawyers: Rethinking the Nature of Legal Services* (Oxford University Press, 2008), Chapter 1.

nation's health? Is it because they are bad for politicians' health? Is it simply the cost? Or is it a combination of these factors? Certainly, one plausible explanation for the downgrading of civil justice is the apparently unstoppable expansion of criminal justice, criminal legal aid and the cost of the penal system.

Criminal legal aid and the battle for resources

A central problem for the Ministry of Justice (and its previous incarnations) since the mid-1980s has been the rapidly rising cost of legal aid and, in particular, the cost of legal aid in criminal cases.[13] Since its establishment in 1949 as a foundational element in the welfare state, the underlying philosophy of civil legal aid has been meaningful access to justice so that the weak and powerless are able to protect their rights in the same way as the strong and powerful. In the criminal justice context, legal representation is considered necessary to ensure fairness for citizens prosecuted by the State with all of its resources. Since the incorporation of the European Convention on Human Rights (ECHR) into English Law in the Human Rights Act 1998, compliance with Article 6 virtually requires the provision of representation at public expense for defendants in the criminal process.

The history of legal aid expenditure has been of gradual and then exponential increases. For most of its

---

[13] www.dca.gov.uk/laid/laid-part1.pdf, paras 2.13–2.15.

history, expenditure on legal aid was not constrained by a fixed budget, and although the Conservative government in the mid-1980s became alarmed at the increase in the legal aid bill, the system had always been 'demand led' until the (interestingly named) Access to Justice Act 1999, when the Labour government introduced a fixed budget for legal aid and with a stroke of the pen abolished legal aid for most civil cases. In tough times, it is inevitably the civil side that suffers the cut. No-win, no-fee arrangements, which had been a helpful supplement to legal aid, overnight supplanted civil legal aid. They became the only option for prospective litigants if they could not afford to pay for legal services, although such arrangements are available only if lawyers are prepared to bear the financial risk of pressing the case.

The increase in the legal aid bill, which had been rising steadily throughout the 1980s, by the late 1990s had started to look uncontrollable. This was not helped by criminal justice policy involving an extensive criminal legislative programme, greater emphasis on detection and enforcement, a 'rebalancing' of the criminal justice system to try to convict more defendants,[14] promotion of stronger crime-control policies and emphasis on custodial sentences. While these policies may be entirely appropriate for criminal justice objectives, in a fixed justice budget that has to accommodate both the rising cost of criminal justice and the civil justice system, it is civil justice that gets squeezed. There are plenty of votes in crime, but few in civil justice. No government ever

---

[14] *Justice for All*, White Paper (The Stationery Office, 2002), Cm 5563, p. 12.

won or lost an election on its record on civil justice. Most members of the public have a detailed view about what the government should be doing about crime, but find it difficult even to visualise what might happen in a civil court.

The relationship between civil and criminal justice and between civil and criminal legal aid historically has not received much attention. Indeed, they are almost never talked about together. References to the 'justice system' and justice system discourse conventionally relate to criminal justice. An interesting exception to this general rule, however, occurred in 2004–5. Concerned about dwindling civil legal aid, the Constitutional Affairs Committee conducted an inquiry into civil legal aid and, for the first time, talked explicitly about the 'squeezing out' of civil legal aid by criminal legal aid and asylum cases.

> Provision for civil legal aid has been squeezed by the twin pressures of the Government's reluctance to devote more money to legal aid and the growth in criminal legal aid, as well as the cost of asylum cases. Whatever action the Government may take to reduce the financial impact of asylum cases on the legal aid system, it is likely that the growth in criminal legal aid will continue to be a burden. The Government should ring fence the civil and criminal legal aid budgets so that the funding for civil work is protected (as immigration work is) and considered quite separately from criminal defence funding.[15]

---

[15] House of Commons Constitutional Affairs Committee, *Civil Legal Aid: Adequacy of Provision*, Fourth Report of Session 2003–04, Vol. 1, HC 391–I, 'conclusions and recommendations', p. 43, para. 1.

A year later, the DCA published its response, entitled 'A fairer deal for legal aid'. For the first time, the government focused specifically on the relationship between spending on criminal legal aid and civil legal aid, acknowledging that an increase in spending on criminal legal aid inevitably reduces the availability of money for advice and representation for civil cases.

> In recent years ... the legal aid scheme has become increasingly focused on providing advice and representation to those facing criminal charges ... expenditure on criminal defence services has risen. This is in sharp contrast to the spend on civil legal aid which has decreased in real terms over the same period [with the exception of child care proceedings and asylum.][16]

Graphs in the paper revealed patterns of expenditure on legal aid and the disproportion between criminal and civil (Figure 2.6).[17] Between 1997 and 2005 expenditure on civil legal aid *had fallen* by a quarter in real terms whereas spending on criminal matters *had increased* by 37 per cent in real terms. The government set out clearly the problem:

> Like all areas of public expenditure, legal aid has to live within an overall budget and the demands on the scheme must be met from within that budget. The growth in criminal spending has meant we have had to reduce the spending on civil, particularly on legal help, and family legal aid, which is undesirable for society as a whole ...

[16] *A Fairer Deal for Legal Aid* (Department for Constitutional Affairs, July 2005), Cm 6591, para. 2.14.
[17] Ibid, paras 2.17–2.18.

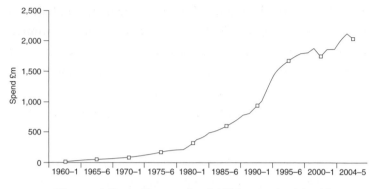

Figure 2.6 Expenditure on Legal Aid (2005 prices) (cash)

Source: Legal Aid Board/Legal Service Commission

Over this period there have been significant increases in spending on the Criminal Justice System as a whole – the police, Crown Prosecution Service, probation and the prison service. Since 1998–99 the cost of the CJS has grown by over 46 per cent, in real terms, driven by Government policy to tackle persistent offending and anti-social behaviour, and to increase the number of offenders brought to justice.[18]

Despite the social importance of the civil justice system to the economy and social order, in a climate of strained resources it is essentially undefended. Although some scholars[19] have valiantly sought to promote the salience of Article 6 of the Human Rights Act to civil procedure, it is undeniable that civil justice process has less explicit protection for its

---

[18] Ibid, Figure 5.

[19] J.M. Jacob, *Civil Justice in the Age of Human Rights* (Ashgate, 2007).

procedures from the Human Rights Act than criminal justice. Most importantly, the civil justice system has few friends in government, since it is through civil cases that the government is directly challenged. Indeed, the inclusion of judicial review within the civil justice 'tent' might be seen as a particular disadvantage for those interested in securing greater resources for civil justice.

> To some extent, the judicial system's ability to process cases is a zero-sum game; as resources are used for one case they are not available for another. If a certain type of case is assured priority, that guarantee can easily have a disproportionate impact on other types of cases. In most courts, criminal cases are understandably granted priority.[20]

It seems that the crisis rhetoric and jaundiced view of civil justice noted in the USA has been replicated in England and reinforced by politicians seeking, reasonably, to control legal aid expenditure. I believe that the 'crisis' in civil justice in the mid-1990s was less some new and unexpected crisis of access to civil justice, but at least in part the result of an accelerating crisis in the justice budget, propelled principally by a growth in criminal justice and criminal legal aid. There was a need for government to restrain justice expenditure and the response was to squeeze civil justice and civil legal aid.

---

[20] R.L. Marcus, 'Malaise of the litigation superpower', Chapter 3 in A.A.S. Zuckerman (ed.), *Civil Justice in Crisis: Comparative Perspectives of Civil Procedure* (Oxford University Press, 1999).

In order to lay the ground for the changes made to legal aid by the 1999 Access to Justice Act – which did many things but increasing access to justice was not one of them – the Lord Chancellor, Lord Irvine, consciously transformed the discourse surrounding legal aid. Legal aid was no longer to be envisioned as a welfare benefit for the poor, helping them to make rights and entitlements effective. Instead it was presented as a gravy train for 'fat-cat lawyers' who were greedily stuffing their pockets with taxpayers' money.[21] While it is politically risky to control expenditure on a welfare benefit, it is easy to take money out of the pockets of avaricious lawyers. In the discourse surrounding unaffordable legal aid, compensation culture and fat-cat lawyers, civil justice and judicial determination became vulnerable. The DCA had to balance its books and investment in the civil courts started to dry up.

The creation of the Ministry of Justice in 2007, bringing prisons, criminal justice, civil justice and the tribunals service under the same roof, has only entrenched the problem of securing sufficient resources for the civil justice system. The preoccupations of the new Ministry are instantly evident from a visit to its website and a brief search through the speeches of ministers and current research. The dominance of

---

[21] See for example the *Daily Telegraph*, Wednesday 29 April 1998 containing an article with the headline 'Irvine names the "fat cats" of legal aid'. The article concerned information provided to Parliament by the then Lord Chancellor, Lord Irvine of Lairg. It states: 'Details of the largest earnings from legal aid were given to Parliament as part of what was seen as a campaign by ministers to justify their far-reaching plans to reform the system.'

crime is everywhere. Civil justice, which has historically been something of a poor relation to crime, has only a shadowy, vestigial presence. As will be argued in the next chapter, in this context the government's adoption of anti-court, pro-diversion policies for civil cases seems self-serving.

The decline of the civil courts

Criminal justice is about the state controlling its citizens. Civil justice, in stark contrast, is mobilised by a vast range of claimants including individual citizens, small and large businesses, institutional claimants and individual citizens calling the state to account. The criminal courts are not paid for by those who use the courts but are supported by the taxpayer through the Treasury and the settlement given to the Ministry of Justice as a result of regular comprehensive spending reviews. Lord Justice Thomas in a wide-ranging lecture on local justice has suggested that the justification for this arrangement arises from the fact that the State has such a clear interest in the maintenance of law and order that 'it has never been in doubt that the state should pay for the provision of the criminal courts'.[22] However, as he goes on to remark, the question of the financing of civil justice 'is quite different and of acute current debate'.

Historically the civil courts were financed jointly by the taxpayer – who paid for judges and court buildings – while

[22] Lord Justice Thomas, Senior Presiding Judge of England and Wales, *The Maintenance of Local Justice*, The Sir Elwyn Jones Memorial Lecture, Bangor University, October 2004, p. 4, www.judiciary.gov.uk/docs/ bangor_university.pdf

the rest of the cost of civil justice was met out of court fees. As Sir Henry Brooke noted in a recent report on the civil courts, this arrangement was based on a number of principles, set out by the Lord Chancellor, Lord Gardiner, in a letter to the Treasury in 1965:

(i) Justice in this country is something in which all the Queen's subjects have an interest, whether it be criminal or civil.

(ii) The courts are for the benefit of all, whether the individual resorts to them or not.

(iii) In the case of the civil courts the citizen benefits from the interpretation of the law by the Judges and from the resolution of disputes, whether between the State and the individual or between individuals.[23]

This policy, however, began to change in the mid-1980s when the government moved to recover the cost of court buildings through court fees, apparently on the assumption that county court proceedings were likely to rise.[24] In 1992, however, the most significant change took place. The Treasury adopted a different view of civil justice. Like any other government service supplied to paying customers,

---

[23] Sir Henry Brooke, *Should the Civil Courts be Unified?* (Judicial Office, August 2008), p. 29, para. 69, www.judiciary.gov.uk/docs/pub_media/brooke_report_ucc.pdf

[24] Sir Henry Brooke wonders whether, even if this prediction was accurate, there was ever any reasonable likelihood that the income from court fees would be capable of covering the investment necessary in court buildings and information technology (IT) over the following twenty years.

the civil justice system was, apparently, thereafter to pay for itself. The entire cost, including the cost of the judges, was to be met from court fees. In his report, Sir Henry notes that this alteration to the funding of a critical social institution was neither debated nor approved by Parliament at the time. Nor, he argues, has it ever been accepted by the senior judiciary. Moreover, as Sir Henry points out, 'in all comparable common law countries, the cost of resourcing the civil courts is shared between the taxpayer and the litigant'.[25] In this connection, Lord Justice Thomas has raised similar concerns about the lack of public debate about the interest of the State in civil justice and whether or not the State should contribute to its provision.[26]

Once the justice system is packaged as a public service as opposed to an arm of government it becomes necessary for it to justify its claims to resources. As Bell argues, in the past the judicial system was seen as one of the natural areas of government activity, like lawmaking, policing and the military, expenditure on which required little justification.[27] But now it has to compete, despite the fact that the social benefit of the civil justice system is difficult to quantify in terms comprehensible by the Treasury. Other jurisdictions, by contrast, accept the principle that the justice system is a public good that should be provided by government.[28] The

---

[25] Sir Henry Brooke, *Should the Civil Courts be Unified?*, p. 30 fn. 74.

[26] Lord Justice Thomas, ibid, p. 4.

[27] J. Bell, *Judiciaries Within Europe: A Comparative Review* (Cambridge University Press, 2006), pp. 376–7.

[28] Public goods are those where one person's consumption does not reduce consumption by others and where it is not possible to exclude

Australian government has recently reviewed and reaffirmed its commitment to supporting civil justice as a public good.[29] Clearly, this is a view that the British government has not shared at least since 1992. But what is truly extraordinary is that, according to Sir Henry's report, figures from HM Courts Service in 2006 revealed that civil justice was producing a profit of over £30 million, which was diverted elsewhere – presumably into the gaping maw of criminal justice. In the year 2006–7, according to Sir Henry,[30] despite this substantial operating profit on civil business, the court service imposed further financial cuts on the civil courts, which are now quite evidently in a state of decline.

Some members of the senior judiciary have been defending boldly the significance of civil justice and trying to publicise the degradation of the civil courts and the problems facing the civil justice system in attempting to provide a modern, professional service to litigants who wish to bring their disputes for resolution. Sir Henry has been a consistent

individuals from access (for example, national defence). These goods tend not to be produced in private markets because people can consume the good without paying for them. Australian Government Productivity Commission, *Report on Government Services, 2008*, Chapter 1, Introduction.

[29] Ibid, Vol. 1, part C. Interestingly, although the authors of the report were able to draw a comprehensive diagram of the criminal justice system (p. C4), they were unable to do so for civil justice. The space assigned to the diagram of civil justice is left blank in the published report, accompanied by the statement that 'a simplified model of the flows through the civil justice system is yet to be developed for this Report' (p. C5).

[30] Sir Henry Brooke, *Should the Civil Courts be Unified?*, para. 75.

voice in this debate. In a lecture in 2006 entitled 'The Future of Civil Justice',[31] he argued that the 'glory' of the civil justice system as a place offering access to the weak had ended as a result of the criminal legal aid overspend.

> For over a hundred years the taxpayer provided a subsidy by paying for the court buildings and the judges. For 40 years he also provided a cushion for those of moderate means so that they could afford to access justice without fear of bankruptcy. All that has ended because of the criminal legal aid overspend and the Treasury's insistence that the Department must itself fund the overspend.[32]

Complaining in 2003 of the lack of resources for a decent building for the commercial court, Lord Mance pointed out that although the specialist courts in the High Court are not as newsworthy or politically sensitive as the criminal courts, they perform a critical social and economic role in supporting the City and service industries and contributing to the economic health of society, that has been overlooked and taken for granted.[33] He also attacked the principle of full cost fee recovery as 'unfair and ill-advised' given that the court

---

[31] 'The future of civil justice: an Address to the Civil Court Users Association' (26 March 2006) www.judiciary.gov.uk/publications_media/speeches/2006/sp260306.htm

[32] Ibid.

[33] Lord Justice Mance, 'Is civil justice a poor relation? The Royal Courts of Justice – loss leader or bankrupt building?', Speech to the London Solicitors Litigation Association Conference, 30 October 2003, www.dca.gov.uk/judicial/speeches/ljm301003.htm

system underpins a wide range of commercial, industrial and
personal transactions and activities.

> Most of these never get near court, for the very good
> reasons that the system is there in case of need, and a
> relatively small number of prior decisions have established
> principles that make fresh litigation unnecessary. There
> is a wider social benefit derived from an established
> justice system, which makes it inequitable and counter-
> productive to place the whole burden on those particular
> litigants who actually end up before a court. In other
> Commonwealth countries, New Zealand and Australia, fee
> income pays for less than half the cost of civil and family
> courts.[34]

The annual reports of Designated Civil Judges provide considerable evidence of the declining standards in
county courts, in terms of the fabric of the buildings, the
pressures on the judiciary and inadequate standards of
administrative support. The Manchester and Bolton Group
County Court Designated Civil Judge recorded in his Annual
Report for 2006–7 that, 'Whatever the statistics may show,
the court operations are creaking at the seams. Morale is also
low … The fact remains that, since court fees generate a sur-
plus, court users are entitled to expect that the fee income be
used to improve services in the civil arena rather than being
diverted to other aspects of the court system such as criminal legal aid.'[35] In February 2007, the Senior Circuit Judge at

---

[34] Ibid.
[35] p. 4, www.hmcourts-service.gov.uk/docs/annualreports_county06_07/
Manchester-Bolton-Group-2006–2007.pdf

London's busiest county court, Judge Paul Collins, received wide press coverage when he complained on BBC radio that the county courts system was in 'chaos'. He blamed a shortage of resources for what he saw as a real risk of 'collapse' in the service.

Having spent time over the past twenty years conducting research in civil courts and tribunals, I can confirm the sorry state of the civil courts. When I talk of the crumbling of civil justice I speak as someone who enters the court buildings through the front door with the litigants and I walk the public corridors. I have personally witnessed the decline. Inadequate information technology; stressed administrative staff; too few books for the judiciary; rushed listing; and judges required to wander down to waiting rooms to collect their next case because there is no one else to do it for them. This is not about lawyers' fees. It is about the resources allocated to the courts. The public areas of some civil courts are run down and squalid. They resemble the worst to be found in NHS hospitals. But the courts are not outpatients' departments. They are sites of justice. They must have authority and legitimacy for which they have to command public confidence and respect.

And the question then is: Does this matter? Should we be concerned about the decline in trials and the degradation of the civil courts? Or is it something to be welcomed as a sign of a healthier society that resolves its conflicts without the intervention of the judiciary and without judicial determination? Is all of this, in fact, a socially positive development? These are questions to which I return in the following chapters.

The contribution of civil justice reviews to declining civil justice

What, then, of the reviews of civil justice of the last decade undertaken around the world in the wake of global civil justice crises? First, most were done quickly and without the benefit of research. The absence of an empirical evidence base on which to formulate proposals for change suggests that governments and law reform commissions had already made up their minds about what the problems with civil justice were and how such perceived problems should be addressed. Few of the reviews set out comprehensive reasons for their existence. Some took it for granted that the civil courts were in need of modernisation or overhaul, the general complaint being that they were too slow, too complicated and too expensive. But in so far as justifications for the reviews were given, they were often confused.

Lord Woolf's review of English civil justice 1994–6 began as an exercise in simplifying the rules of court. Complaints about the civil courts were not new. They had been trundling along since the time of Dickens, if not Shakespeare. But it is difficult to see why, exactly, a sense of impending crisis seemed to occur in 1994 when the reforming Conservative Lord Chancellor, James Mackay, asked Lord Woolf to develop unified rules of court and then to undertake a review of civil justice. Civil servants in the Lord Chancellor's Department involved in the discussions preceding the review remember no immediate crisis – rather a sense that Britain was lagging behind some other jurisdictions that had already undertaken reviews and that the Department needed to take a fundamental look at expenditure and, in particular, expenditure on legal aid.[36]

The Introduction to Lord Woolf's *Interim Report*, published in 1995, sets out the perceived problems of civil justice. The report is called 'Access to Justice',[37] but the narrative precisely reflects the two competing stories about civil justice in the late twentieth century – too little access, too much litigation. On the one hand the report seeks to break down barriers to justice, while on the other it sends a clear message that diversion and settlement is the goal, that courts exist only as a last resort and, perhaps, as a symbol of failure. The problems of civil justice are said to be cost, complexity and delay and blame for these problems is laid principally at the feet of lawyers. Indeed, the *Interim Report* is infused with anti-lawyer rhetoric.[38] There are copious references to excessively adversarial tactics ('no control of their worst excesses'; 'a battlefield where no rules apply'); reasonable timetables defeated by tactical gamesmanship ('the rules are flouted on a vast scale'); intentional delay that only serves the interests of lawyers; courts that are powerless in the face of aggressive adversarialism ('the powers of the courts have fallen behind the more sophisticated and aggressive tactics of some litigators'[39]); subversion of procedural

---

[36] In conversation with civil servants involved in the review, it was said that 'the courts had become an embarrassment. In comparison with Australia and the USA, the English courts were rather C19th, lacking energy and purpose. They represented a judicial gymnasium demonstrating the Athenian school of rhetoric'.

[37] Lord Woolf, *Access to Justice, Interim Report* (Lord Chancellor's Department, 1995), Chapter 3, 'The problems and their causes'.

[38] Ibid, paras 4–6.

[39] Ibid, para. 7.

rules ('whether by incompetence or deliberation'[40]); delay is of more benefit to legal advisers than to parties, allowing lawyers to 'carry excessive caseloads in which the minimum possible action occurs over the maximum possible timescale'.[41] Moreover, there is collusion between opposing sides as the legal advisers 'indulge' each other's 'misdemeanours'.[42] What we are presented with is a vision of both litigants and the justice system at the mercy of incompetent and/or aggressive lawyers who act only in their own interest. It is a manifestation of the weakness of the Law Society at the time that this anti-lawyer polemic was accepted without comment and indeed enthusiastically welcomed by the profession.[43] The clear message of the Report is that litigation and adjudication are bad and disagreeable, while settlement and, in particular, ADR are attractive and in everyone's best interests. The ascendance of ADR in the Woolf report and its worldwide adoption is the subject of the next chapter.

However, the Report also talks about the need for the courts to be slick and smooth in order to compete for international commercial business. It recognises the role of English civil justice as an invisible export and an important income stream for the City of London. But the Report is never clear, and it does not itself seem to be sure, which principal audience

[40] Ibid, para. 8.
[41] Ibid, para. 31.
[42] Ibid, para. 31.
[43] The only voice consistently raised against the arguments in the Woolf report was Professor Michael Zander. See articles and speeches by M. Zander 1995–6, 'Why the Woolf reforms won't work', M. Zander QC, 'The state of justice', 51st Hamlyn Lectures, 1999.

it is addressing or whether it is for or against access to the courts.

Lord Woolf's solution to the perceived problems of civil justice was to promote settlement at the earliest moment and preferably without the issue of court proceedings. The judiciary were to become case managers responsible for rationing procedure, guided by principles of efficiency, equality of arms and expedition. This transformation and its implications are the subject of Chapter 4. The purpose of the new system was to provide a last rather than first resort for those in dispute. The intention was that cases should be settled privately and without the need to issue proceedings in court. Where proceedings had to be issued, cases should be settled as quickly as possible between the parties. Thus a principal solution to the notional crisis in civil justice was diversion of cases from the courts through early ADR and pre-action protocols. For those litigants who insisted on issuing proceedings in court, there would be proactive judicial case management, stripped-down procedures, reduction in orality, more emphasis on writing and strict timetables. Judges were given the power to divert cases to ADR[44] and penalties could be imposed on litigants who 'unreasonably' insisted on going to trial rather than attempting ADR.[45] By raising the financial limit on the small claims jurisdiction, a large proportion of county court business was pushed down into an informal, non-public procedure operated by District Judges

---

[44] Civil Procedure Rules R26.4.
[45] Factors to be taken into account when deciding costs issues include 'the efforts made, if any, before and during the proceedings in order to try and resolve the dispute' (Parts 1 and 44 Civil Procedure Rules).

in chambers, thus removing from visibility an enormous volume of judicial determinations.[46]

Lord Woolf's intention was to reduce delay, complexity and cost in the civil justice system. The evidence suggests that post-issue delay has been reduced and that cases are being settled earlier.[47] The concept of 'proportionality' in procedure has also been a constructive improvement to the operation of civil justice. However, the evidence also suggests that at least two of the objectives have not been met. The Civil Procedural Rules have become increasingly elaborate over the decade since they were introduced and the cost of litigation has risen.[48] Indeed, in 2008, the head of civil justice, Sir Anthony Clarke MR, announced the appointment of Lord Justice Jackson to undertake a one-year fundamental review

[46] In this connection it is interesting to note that in recent years Ministry of Justice ADR policy has focused increasing attention on trying to persuade small claims litigants to mediate their claims on the telephone rather than coming to court.

[47] *Further Findings: A Continuing Evaluation of the Civil Justice Reforms* (Department for Constitutional Affairs, 2002), sections 3 and 6.

[48] P. Fenn, N. Rickman and D. Vencappa, 'The impact of the Woolf reforms on costs and delay' (2009), www.nottingham.ac.uk/business/cris/papers/2009–1.pdf. Analysing a large dataset, the authors conclude: '[T]he Woolf reforms of April 1999 may have achieved its objective in reducing delay in the settlement of litigated claims. However, this achievement may have been bought at the expense of an apparent increase in the delay in settling claims pre-issue (the majority of all cases). At the same time, after controlling for these changes in case duration, it seems that overall case costs have increased substantially over pre-2000 costs for cases of comparable value … There may of course be other factors at work in this period, but the weight of evidence does at least suggest that the Woolf reforms are a plausible candidate explanation.'

of the rules and principles governing the costs of civil litigation, commencing in January 2009. The objective of the review was 'to make recommendations in order to promote access to justice at proportionate cost'.[49] The preliminary report of Lord Justice Jackson's costs review, published in May 2009, confirms the view that costs of litigation have increased:

> [I]t must be accepted that some of the cost increases since 1999 do appear to be consequential upon the Woolf reforms. Pre-action protocols and the requirements of the CPR [Civil Procedure Rules] have led to 'front loading' of costs. Also the detailed requirements of the CPR and the case management orders of courts cause parties to incur costs which would not have been incurred pre April 1999. Where cases settle between issue and trial (and the vast majority of cases do so settle) the costs of achieving settlement are sometimes higher than before.[50]

What the reforms have succeeded in doing, however, is removing cases from the justice system. Although the number of people attempting ADR has not been particularly significant, the rate of issue has gone down in both the county court and the High Court and the number of trials has reduced. The only area of increase in judicial determination is in small claims, and the pressure here is clearly visible. While the courts may be dark, the offices of District Judges are heaving.

---

[49] The announcement appeared on the Judicial Office website where the terms of reference for the review are available at www.judiciary.gov.uk/about_judiciary/cost-review/tor.htm

[50] Lord Justice Jackson, *Civil Litigation Costs Review, Preliminary Report* (Judicial Office, 8 May 2009).

Although Lord Woolf did not talk about pressure on resources in his report, it is clear that this was a principal reason why the Lord Chancellor's Department commissioned the review. Whatever Lord Woolf's intention, and certainly he did not intend civil justice to be subsequently starved of resources, it has to be accepted that the terms of the argument and the language of the *Interim* and *Final Reports* were available to be used by government to support and justify squeezing resources for the civil courts. If settlement is the principal aim of civil justice, and private dispute resolution the new way of getting there, what matter if the civil courts are short of money?

Other civil justice reviews around the world in the mid-1990s used similar crisis rhetoric, but explicitly in the context of cost pressures on justice budgets. What we find as an accepted principle is the need to control expenditure on civil justice occurring in happy coincidence with the development of the contemporary ADR movement. In 1996, the Canadian Bar Association Task Force on Civil Justice announced that Canada's civil justice system was functioning under 'ever-increasing pressures. The pressures include reduced funding and dwindling resources at both the national and the provincial level and increased demands on the system'.[51]

In 1996 the Ontario Ministry of Justice published a review of civil justice. The review had been set up in 1994 as a joint initiative by the judiciary and the Attorney General. The review's mandate was 'to develop an overall strategy for the civil justice system in an effort to provide a speedier, more streamlined

---

[51] Civil Justice Reform Working Group, *Effective and Affordable Civil Justice* (Justice Review Task Force, 2006), para. 2.4, p. 4.

and more efficient structure which will maximize the utilization of public resources allocated to civil justice'. Key components of the First Report, released in March 1995, were the transformation of courts into 'dispute resolution centres' adopting a 'multi-door' concept of dispute resolution and integrating ADR, a case flow management system that will process cases in accordance with prescribed time parameters using a team approach, a unified management, administrative and budgetary structure with clear lines of accountability, and better use of technology.

In the 1990s, Australia underwent a stream of federal and state civil justice reviews. Writing in 1999 about those civil justice reforms, Ted Wright suggests that at least part of the stimulus for this fascination with civil justice reform was the government's need to reduce spending on courts and legal aid, and a sense of crisis among the judiciary in the face of burgeoning caseloads.[52]

In Hong Kong the Chief Justice established a working party in 2000 to conduct a similar civil justice review. The findings were published in 2004.[53] Although the Hong Kong approach to reform was much influenced by the Woolf reforms, there was a conscious attempt to avoid some of the pitfalls that had been observed with the implementation of these reforms. The Hong Kong committee reviewed the impact of the Woolf reforms and doubted whether the objectives of the reforms had been achieved in terms of cost or complexity.

[52] T. Wright, 'Australia: a need for clarity', *Justice System Journal*, Special Issue on Understanding Civil Justice Reform in Anglo–American Legal Systems, 20 (1999), 131.
[53] Chief Justice's Working Party on Civil Justice Reform, *Civil Justice Reform: Final Report* (Hong Kong Judiciary, 2004).

They felt that the new civil procedure rules had not turned out to be as user friendly as hoped. The White Book was now similar in size and complexity to the pre-CPR White Book. They were also concerned about the 'front-loading' of cases. The approach of the Hong Kong working party therefore was to find ways of simplifying procedures, doing more on paper and discouraging over-elaboration and oral evidence. Nonetheless, they also sought to foster greater openness and encourage earlier settlements 'giving proper consideration to alternative modes of dispute resolution'. Unlike other civil justice reviews, the Hong Kong working party was not in favour of proactivity by the court. 'The case management powers are there to curb the excesses of the adversarial system, not to displace that system.'[54] Hong Kong, in many respects, runs against the tide of civil justice reviews. It is more moderate, less ambitious and more sceptical about moving towards activist courts. Its ruminations on ADR are also somewhat more tentative than elsewhere. The reforms, implemented on 2 April 2009, are supported by 'underlying objectives', which are to increase the cost-effectiveness of practice and procedure, to ensure cases are dealt with as expeditiously as is reasonably practicable, to promote a sense of reasonable proportion and procedural economy in the conduct of proceedings, to ensure fairness between the parties, to facilitate the settlement of disputes and to ensure that the resources of the Court are distributed fairly.[55]

[54] Ibid, para. 109, p. 55.
[55] Ibid, p. 56.

There are other reviews that have built on Lord Woolf's reforms. A good example is the review of civil justice conducted in British Columbia whose report was published in November 2006.[56] The review report promotes a strong emphasis on access to justice and proportionality. The most recent civil justice review, and perhaps the most sophisticated and comprehensive, is yet another Australian report by the Victorian Law Reform Commission, published in May 2008. The review was established in May 2004, after the Attorney General of Victoria issued a Justice Statement outlining directions for the reform of Victoria's justice system. Objectives were to streamline litigation processes, reduce costs and court delays and achieve greater uniformity between different courts. The Justice Statement identified the need for modernisation, simplification and harmonisation of the rules and civil procedure within and across the jurisdictions of the various civil courts; reduction in the cost of litigation; promotion of the principle of fairness, timeliness, proportionality, choice, transparency, quality, efficiency and accountability in the civil justice system. One innovative feature of the Victoria reforms was to place a new 'overriding responsibility' on the parties to litigation and their lawyers to comply with ethical obligations relating to truth telling, honesty and efficiency. However, despite the evident care and thought that went into the review, and the attempt to specify goals of the civil justice system, the Commission's final report identifies the goals of civil justice almost entirely in relation to process, with little

---

[56] Civil Justice Reform Working Group, *Effective and Affordable Civil Justice* (Vancouver: Justice Review Task Force, 2006).

discussion of either the purpose of civil justice or desirable outcomes.[57]

Policy making in the dark

A worrying feature of the civil justice reviews around the world was that they were in all cases conducted and concluded in the absence of any research or understanding of the dynamics of civil justice, or even a convincing description of the work of the courts and the magnitude of cost and delay. Most proceeded on the basis of anecdote and the partial views of different actors within justice systems (legal professionals, judiciary and litigants). The British Columbia civil justice review report pointed out that no formal studies had been found showing empirical data on the cost, delay and complexity of litigation in BC. It noted that a similar problem had been faced by the Ontario civil justice review. Indeed, the Ontario review report expressed surprise at the lack of available evidence to support the work of the review body, stating that 'on such an important issue, one would expect to find a wealth of research. Surprisingly, there is little analysis or hard data available. This is true not only for Ontario but for most jurisdictions around the world'.[58]

[57] The key 'goals' specified for civil justice were accessibility, affordability, equality of arms, proportionality, consistency, predictability and timeliness, although 'getting to the truth' was also included in the list. *Civil Justice Review, Report 14* (Victorian Law Reform Commission, 28 May 2008), www.lawreform.vic.gov.au/wps/wcm/connect/Law+Reform/resources/file/ebbd1209a2983c2/

[58] Quoted in the British Columbia Civil Justice Review, *Effective and Affordable Civil Justice*.

The Victoria civil justice review in 2008 remarked that despite frequent criticisms of civil justice, solutions to the problems seemed to be elusive and that evidence to help understand the problems was lacking: 'There is relatively little empirical data with which to assess the overall magnitude of the problems, the causal explanations for the problems, or the impact of reforms.' Equally importantly, it points out that the process of successful review and reform must be ongoing and iterative. 'Adequate empirical data and appropriate measures of performance and feedback from key participants in the process, including regular users of the court system, are necessary if reform is to be effective.'[59] In this context, the report deplores the absence of quantitative or qualitative research on the operation of the current civil justice system, 'let alone rigorous attempts to measure the impact of changes'. Indeed, the report emphasises the fact that there has been relatively little Australian research on whether recent civil procedural reforms have even achieved their stated goals of improving efficiency.[60]

It is remarkable how willing governments around the world have been to assert the existence of crises and propose solutions without any evidence base or means of assessing the effect of the reforms on access to justice, on different types of litigants or on the judiciary. Nor does there seem to have been much investment in research that might establish the extent to which the reforms have met their objectives.

---

[59] Victorian Law Reform Commission Report, p. 10.
[60] Ibid, p. 99.

In England, the Inquiry on Access to Justice contained bold statements about the problems endemic in the civil justice system that Lord Woolf was seeking to overcome in his programme of reform. But the polemic of the *Interim Report* was supported principally by anecdotal evidence[61] combined with fragments of research material drawn from a number of different sources. The Inquiry had not been allocated a budget for research, and in any case, the timescale set for the Inquiry effectively precluded the possibility that the team could collect large-scale data about the operation of the civil justice system. It is possible that this was not seen as a weakness in the approach since there was, apparently, a shared or common understanding of what the problems were. Much of Lord Woolf's diagnosis had to be taken on trust, but part of the reason why it *was* taken on trust was that many of the assertions and arguments in the report resonated at least with the *worst* experiences of litigants, practitioners and the judiciary. The Woolf road shows, held at different locations around the country as part of the Inquiry process, provided a platform for harried litigants to explain how their lives had been ruined by litigation. Affecting though these personal stories were, what was lacking from the Woolf discourse was any sense of

---

[61] 'A number of businesses have told me …' (para. 13, *Interim Report*); 'I stress this last point because it was made so forcefully to me by representatives of professional and commercial concerns which find themselves involved in litigation' (para. 14, *Interim Report*); 'Many of those who make their living by conducting litigation accepted at the seminars that they would not be able to afford their own services if they had the misfortune to be caught up in legal proceedings' (para. 17, *Interim Report*).

the *average*, the *usual* or the wider context of litigation in the courts.

Although no large-scale research exercise was undertaken to support the Woolf Inquiry, a subsequent piece of research was commissioned by the Lord Chancellor's Department (LCD) to provide baseline information about litigation in the county courts *prior* to the implementation of Lord Woolf's reforms. Focusing on defended cases above the small claims limit at the time (£3,000), the study provides basic information about the subject matter, parties, case values, length and outcomes of the caseload in seven county courts in England during the period August 1998 to February 1999.[62] It also provides a sketchy impression of legal costs.

The research reveals the domination of personal injury (PI) cases in the caseloads of the county courts – between half and 80 per cent of county court defended cases – with breach of contract, goods and services and debt cases accounting for most of the remainder. While in PI cases individuals were generally suing insurance companies or public bodies, the majority of claimants in non-PI cases were businesses or public bodies suing either each other or individual defendants. On the whole, the vast majority of defended claims in the

---

[62] H. Genn, 'The Pre-Woolf Litigation Landscape in the County Courts', September 2002, available at www.ucl.ac.uk/laws/genn. The county courts included in the study were Cambridge, Luton, Newcastle, Nottingham, Reading, Worcester and Central London County Court. The results of the study were to have been used as a basis for assessing the effectiveness of the reforms. Some attempt at a comparison has been undertaken by the Ministry of Justice's research unit, although the results have yet to be published.

county courts prior to the Woolf reforms were for modest sums, with *at least* three in four defended non-PI cases coming within the current small-claims or fast-track limit (under £15,000). In most courts the proportion was 85 per cent or more, with the average value of non-PI claims being about £5,000. In both PI and non-PI cases, three-quarters of awards or settlements were for less than £10,000 and half were for less than £5,000.

The research demonstrated the very high settlement rate in PI cases prior to the introduction of the Woolf reforms, with about 90 per cent ending in pre-trial settlement. Among non-PI cases the settlement rate was generally lower, with a higher proportion of trials and a much higher proportion of cases being withdrawn. Debt cases were the most likely of all case types to end in trial (38 per cent) and in all of those cases the claimant succeeded. The highest proportion of cases going to trial occurred where individuals were being sued by corporate or public bodies, thus confirming evidence from elsewhere[63] that private individuals are more likely to be involved in civil trials as defendants than as claimants. In the overwhelming majority of cases going to trial (96 per cent) the claimant succeeded and in all cases where corporate or public bodies sued individuals, the claimant won. In no case did a private individual succeed at trial as a defendant.

Although information about legal costs was difficult to obtain, the study suggests that in non-PI cases at least, the level of legal costs was relatively modest, with many having

[63] H. Genn, *Paths to Justice: What People Think and Do About Going to Law* (Hart, 1999).

costs of below £500. Even in PI cases, about half had costs of around £2,000 or less, and only one-quarter had costs of over £4,000.

The study is valuable for highlighting several issues. Although there was variation in the picture between different courts, the most striking differences found were between PI and non-PI cases. This underscores the difficulty of generalising about 'civil litigation' as a whole. Personal injury actions dominated the defended caseloads of most courts. They overwhelmingly ended in out-of-court settlement rather than trial and tended to take longer to conclude than non-PI cases. Analysis of settlements and awards in PI cases shows that the value of most claims was relatively modest. Non-PI cases were more varied in terms of party configuration and use of legal representation. Non-PI actions were much more likely to be started by corporate or public bodies and defendants were much more likely than in PI cases to be private individuals. Legal representation was patchier and there was a substantial minority of cases in which either the defendant or both sides had no legal representation. In three-quarters of non-PI trials, the defendant was an individual rather than a corporate or public body. Non-PI cases tended to end more quickly than PI cases, but a higher proportion was withdrawn and a larger proportion went on to trial. The average amount of money awarded in settlement or at trial in non-PI cases was remarkably similar to that in PI claims.

The data produced by this pre-Woolf baseline study conflict with some of the more apocalyptic claims and predictions that characterised the discourse of the Woolf debate, perhaps reflecting the dominance of concern about litigation

67

in the High Court as opposed to the everyday stuff of the county courts.

Common solutions

The common solutions that emerged from civil justice reviews around the world were the wholesale introduction of ADR, cost control, stripping down of procedure and active case management by the judiciary to save costs to the justice system and the parties. In all of these reports, the discussion of fundamental reform proceeds with little acknowledgement of any link between procedure, fairness and substantive outcome. With the notable exception of the most recent review in Victoria, there is little sense conveyed that any important social purpose is served by the civil justice system or of any public good to be protected in civil justice. Certainly there is no suggestion that there are cases that should be facilitated into the courts, no sense that time and resources should be made available for particular types or classes of cases. There is no plan. There are no principles other than efficiency. There is no space for substantive justice or the value of adjudication or any indication of the kinds of cases in which adjudication might be especially important. The only cases that are anticipated to proceed to adjudication are those where the lawyers are too incompetent or too greedy to achieve a settlement or the parties are too difficult and short-sighted to agree to a compromise. It may be that Bentham's link between procedural justice and substantive justice was so well understood, so well recognised by the writers and readers of the civil justice reviews around the world that it did not have to be spelled out and the balance between efficiency and substantive justice did not have to be articulated. Yet in a civil justice system in which outcomes are always conceptualised as compromise and settlement rather than adjudication, the value of procedure becomes less and less clear because one is not concerned with standards of evidence and proof. One is not preparing for adjudication. One is simply laying the ground for settlement.

Some commentators have suggested that the driving purpose of such reforms to civil justice has been to provide on the one hand more access, but on the other less justice. Increasing the efficiency of procedures might improve the access of citizens to the courts, but with less certainty about whether the reduced processes were capable of delivering just, accurate outcomes.[64] But in fact it is hard not to draw the conclusion that the main thrust of modern civil justice reform is about neither more access nor more justice. It is simply about diversion of disputants away from the courts. It is essentially about less law and the downgrading of civil justice. This seems to be as true for large commercial cases as for the everyday lower-value problems of citizens. The push for less law is supported by the growing ADR profession interested in gaining a foothold in large commercial litigation.

---

[64] C.M. Hanycz, 'More access to less justice: efficiency, proportionality and costs in Canadian civil justice reform', *Civil Justice Quarterly*, 27:1 (2008), 98–122, arguing that: 'Unfortunately, this fundamental question seems to have been largely ignored not only in Lord Woolf's work, but in the body of scholarship that followed', p. 103.

Access to justice – minding the justice gap

In truth, the phrase itself, 'access to justice', is a profound and powerful expression of a social need which is imperative, urgent and more widespread than is generally acknowledged.[65]

The principle of equal access to the legal system is part of our framework of political legitimacy.[66]

This same decade of interest in civil justice policy has seen a remarkable resurgence of what are called 'legal needs' studies seeking to map the prevalence of legal problems experienced by the public and to chart citizens' responses. This resurgence coincided but was not directly linked with the 'crises' of civil justice and reforms. The question of why there should have been a resurgence of studies in this field is itself interesting. Was it in response to a perceived crisis of access to justice? Was it in response to the anti-law and justice rhetoric of the reviews? Or was it a response to attempts to reform civil justice in the name of the public in the absence of any empirical evidence about the needs, interests or expectations of the public? The most likely explanation is that it was a direct result of pressure on civil legal aid. Part of the underlying purpose of the legal needs studies was to highlight civil justice problems and the unmet need for

---

[65] Sir Jack Jacob, 'Access to justice in England' in Mauro Cappelletti and Bryant Garth (eds), *Access to Justice, Vol 1: a World Survey* (Alphen aan den Rhijn/Milan, 1978), p. 417.

[66] D. Luban, *Lawyers and Justice* (Princeton University Press, 1988), p. 251.

advice and legal representation as funds were being sucked into criminal legal aid.[67]

The premise of most of the legal needs studies in the last decade is that in assessing and reforming civil justice, information about the public's needs and experiences is essential. Certainly the stimulus for my own study, *Paths to Justice*, was concern that the Woolf reforms had formulated reforms on a rather weak, if not absent, evidence base about the reality of access to justice for citizens.[68] *Paths to Justice* was designed to understand, from the bottom up, the relevance of the justice system to the resolution of legal problems that citizens face in their everyday lives. Since then, a number of large-scale general population studies in countries around the world have adopted its broad methodological approach to explore the public's experience of civil justice problems. Most notably, the Legal Services Commission has instituted a regular survey called the English and Welsh Civil and Social Justice Survey (CSJS), which has developed and enhanced the methodology of *Paths to Justice*.[69]

---

[67] Nicola Lacey's identification of the countries in which she has noticed an increasing politicisation of criminal justice and growth in criminalisation and punitive sentencing regimes, maps on well to the places where civil justice crises, reviews and reforms have emerged. Nicola Lacey, *The Prisoners' Dilemma*, 59th Hamlyn Lectures (Cambridge University Press, 2008).

[68] H. Genn, *Paths to Justice*.

[69] First conducted in 2001, the CSJS is now conducted continuously, with an evolving questionnaire that enables gaps in understanding to be addressed on an ongoing basis. The most recent report is P. Pleasence, N.J. Balmer, T. Tam, A. Buck, M. Smith and A. Patel, *Civil Justice in England and Wales: Report of the 2007 English and Welsh Civil and Social Justice Survey* (Legal Services Commission, 2008), LSRC Research Paper

The broad findings of *Paths to Justice* and those that followed around the world were that everyday legal problems are ubiquitous and that the most common strategy adopted by the public is to try to settle their disputes themselves. Moreover, the types of civil justice problems most commonly experienced by the public seem to be similar all around the world: consumer disputes, debt problems, problems with landlords, problems with neighbours, employment problems and problems with benefits. Most importantly, for the earlier discussion of litigation explosions, is that across vastly different cultures there is no evidence of any 'rush to law'. On the contrary, for most types of problems (excluding divorce and separation) involvement in legal proceedings is a rare exception. The studies tell us that when faced with a legal problem what people want is to have an end to the dispute and to get on with their lives. Most people involve themselves in a legal action only because there is a significant issue at stake that threatens their well-being or that of their family. But there is

No. 22. Other examples include: *Consultancy Study on the Demand for and Supply of Legal and Related Services* (Hong Kong Department of Justice, 2008); C. Coumarelos, Z. Wei and A. Zhou, *Justice Made to Measure: NSW legal needs survey in disadvantaged areas* (Law and Justice Foundation of New South Wales, 2006); M. Murayama, 'Experiences of problems and disputing behaviour in Japan', *Meiji Law Journal*, 14 (2007), 1–59; B.C.J. Van Velthoven and M.J. ter Voert, *Geschilbeslechtingsdelta 2003* (WODC, 2004); M. Gramatikov, 'Multiple justiciable problems in Bulgaria' (Tilburg University Legal Studies Working Paper No. 16/2008, 2008). The common approach of these surveys, based on the *Paths to Justice* concept of the 'justiciable event', provides an opportunity to compare public experiences and responses to civil justice problems.

also a lack of knowledge about civil justice and concern about the dangers of becoming involved in its procedures, because of its presumed unpleasantness, expense and unpredictability. To that extent, the jaundiced view of civil justice has been fully internalised by the public, whether or not they have ever had cause to use it. And this is corrosive, since the sense of exclusion from State dispute-resolution processes may lead to frustration, alienation and a sense that the rights and entitlements promised by the State are worthless.

Conclusion

Government policy over the last decade in England (and in other jurisdictions) has led to increased expenditure on criminal justice and created pressure on the justice budget. The response has been to look for savings in civil justice. This has been achieved through a civil reform programme involving diversion of cases away from public courts and into private dispute resolution, stripping down court procedure and making litigants pay for court buildings, judges and the administration, through full cost fee recovery. Civil courts have been starved of resources while the profits from fees have been applied to the criminal courts. These reforms have been facilitated by an anti-justice, anti-adjudication discourse which undermines civil justice and which is internalised by the public, thus alienating them from the protective function of the law and machinery of civil justice. The diversionary pressures on civil cases are indiscriminate rather than strategic. There is no plan other than to encourage as much as possible out of the courts.

Contemporary civil justice policy raises concern about access to justice for individuals, but also the fundamental question of how much and what form of civil justice we need to achieve the purposes of the system in supporting economic activity, civil society and good governance. As Jolowicz has convincingly argued, where the law is well developed, most people for most of the time simply accept it, complying with their legal obligations and respecting the rights of others and that the effectiveness of law depends on the messages that come from the courts.[70]

We have always had a system that combines a high level of settlement with high-quality, authoritative adjudication. But we need public adjudication to ground normative statements and to make them sufficiently clear that citizens and business can abide by the rules and avoid legal risk. An elaborated, granular body of rules in a common law system offers guidance on how to ascertain legal risk, something which, in theory at least, many civil law systems do not possess. Thin law can lead to uncertainty and risk aversion in the commercial world so that economic possibilities are not optimised. Moreover, where there is uncertainty there is fertile ground for disputes to escalate. 'Trials reduce disputes and it is a profound mistake to view a trial as a failure of the civil justice system.' It is not necessarily true that an unsatisfactory settlement is better than the best trial.[71]

---

[70] J.A. Jolowicz, 'On the nature and purposes of civil procedural law' in I.R. Scott (ed.), *International Perspectives on Civil Justice* (Sweet & Maxwell, 1990), pp. 27–45.

[71] P.E. Higginbotham, 'So why do we call them trial courts?', *Southern Methodist University Law Review*, 55 (2002), 1405–21, 1421.

Instead of indiscriminately driving cases away, we should be asking what cases should be facilitated into court and how they should be facilitated. To go back to the snail in the bottle, Mrs Donoghue's case was heard by the House of Lords because she was fortunate to find a solicitor and barrister who would take on her case without payment. In order for the case to be taken to the House of Lords, Mrs Donoghue had to declare herself a pauper.[72] What would have happened to that case today, so important to the development of the tort of negligence, particularly since we are told that even cases involving points of law are suitable for mediation?[73]

Which cases currently, potentially vital to the development of the law, are not reaching formal determination because litigants are being told to take their business elsewhere or because of court fees? And we should question why, when this happens, we have been encouraged to think that this is a success. If we have no plan, then policies may collide. In conversation recently, a court manager mentioned that there had been a significant reduction in the number of care proceedings being issued in court by local authorities. The court fee has risen from £150 to £4,000. As a result, local authorities are holding back because of caps on their own expenditure. They are not proceeding to trial, but instead trying to reach a settlement with parents. This may be a constructive outcome.

[72] M.R. Taylor QC, 'Mrs. Donoghue's journey', amended version of original paper (Scottish Council of Law Reporting, 2004), www.scottishlawreports.org.uk/resources/dvs/mrs-donoghue-journey.html
[73] *Royal Bank of Canada v Secretary of State for Defence* [2003] EWHC 1479.

It might be a socially positive development. But in light of the recent death of Baby P,[74] it might not.

Perhaps the question we should be debating is *how many trials* and in *what kinds of cases* do we need to ensure that civil justice performs its social and economic functions? It is not, as the anti-lawyer joke goes, 'Well Mr Pitkin, you have an excellent case. How much justice can you afford?'[75] The question is how much formal justice do we need to ensure that the common law can be refreshed, that legal risk can be minimised and that disputes can be rapidly resolved when they arise? Or, to put it another way, how much justice can we afford to forego? I do not believe at the moment that anyone is even considering that question, let alone framing policy that would achieve those ends. In fact, I do not believe that there is much in the way of significant policy development in the field of civil justice at all, other than holding down costs. And this was the case long before the current economic crisis. We need a positive understanding of the role and value of the civil justice system. We need a strategy for the cases that we want to encourage into the system and those that we would prefer to discourage and we need to articulate our reasons for both of these choices. Our judgement about the quality of our

[74] A high-profile child-abuse case in November 2008 in which a seventeen- month-old child was killed by his parents. The child had been on the local authority risk register for nine months prior to his death, but no action had been taken by the authority to remove the child from the care of his abusive parents.

[75] This allusion is made by J. Lande, 'How much justice can we afford?: Defining the courts' roles and deciding the appropriate number of trials, settlement signals, and other elements needed to administer justice', *Journal of Dispute Resolution* (2006), 213.

civil justice system should not be measured simply in terms of speed and cheapness, or by how many cases we can persuade to go elsewhere. Finally, we need to re-establish civil justice as a public good, recognising that it has a significant social purpose that is as important to the health of society as criminal justice.

3

ADR and civil justice: what's justice got to do with it?

My starting point for this chapter is essentially the conclusion of the previous chapter: that the civil justice system has a significant social purpose and that the fundamental challenge for reformers is how to provide a modern, efficient system that delivers just outcomes by means of procedures that are fair and that are perceived to be so by litigants and other court users – a system that delivers justice and enjoys public confidence. Most importantly, the question is how the public purpose of the civil justice system – in supporting social and economic stability – is achieved in a climate of strained resources and when the demands of criminal justice seem to be unstoppable. I argued that we have been presented with two competing narratives about civil justice: that there is not enough access to justice and that there is too much litigation. As far as the government and some sections of the judiciary are concerned, the answer to both arguments seems to be diverting cases away from the courts and into private dispute resolution processes and in particular mediation. This trend is true of policy in relation to family disputes, civil and commercial disputes and, more recently, administrative justice disputes involving citizen and State.[1] In this context I am interested in reflecting on who and what is driving ADR policy, and why.

My focus is principally on the promotion of ADR for non-family civil disputes and, in particular, judicial and government policy on mediation. While my interest in civil justice reform has inevitably led to engagement with ADR policy, I have also developed a good ground-floor feel for what mediation offers and for its limitations as a result of having undertaken a number of evaluations of court-annexed mediation schemes in England over the last decade. These evaluations involved talking to litigants who had chosen to mediate, those who had rejected the opportunity to mediate, those who felt they had been forced to mediate and those who would have liked the opportunity to mediate. I have watched mediations. I have talked to lawyers about mediation and to mediators about mediation. I have talked to business people involved in disputes, private individuals involved in disputes and harried litigants in person.

By way of preliminary, therefore, and to be clear, my position on mediation is that it is an important supplement to courts. In my view, mediation has rightly become a feature on the landscape of dispute resolution – an option for anyone

[1] See the Legal Services Consultation Document, A *New Focus For Civil Legal Aid: Encouraging Early Resolution; Discouraging Unnecessary Litigation* (DCA, 2004) and the government response at www.dca. gov.uk/response-litigation.pdf, which focused on family cases and 'discouraging unnecessary publicly-funded litigation'. See also on judicial review, V. Bondy, M. Doyle and V. Reid, 'Mediation and judicial review – mind the research gap', *Judicial Review*, September (2005), www. publiclawproject.org.uk/downloads/MindResGap.pdf

unfortunate enough to have become involved in a civil dispute. I believe that the public and the legal profession should be properly educated about the potential of mediation from the earliest possible moment and I believe that mediation facilities should be made easily available to anyone contemplating litigation. But I have three significant concerns. First, I am equally clear that mediation is most appropriate and successful when the parties enter the process voluntarily. Second, that ADR cannot supplant the machinery of civil justice precisely because, in civil cases, the background threat of litigation is necessary to bring people to the negotiating table. Finally, and most importantly, I am concerned that the case for mediation has routinely been made not so much on the strength of its special benefits but by setting it up in opposition to adjudication and promoting it through anti-adjudication and anti-law discourse. Of course there are elegant advocates who provide much more sophisticated accounts of the purpose and value of mediation,[2] but it is a cruder message that has been picked up by government and used to justify a helpfully economical policy of diverting cases away from courts.

What is ADR?

Alternative dispute resolution is an umbrella term which is generally applied to a range of techniques for resolving disputes other than by means of traditional court adjudication – for example mediation, early neutral evaluation, arbitration,

---

[2] An obvious and convincing advocate is Carrie Menkel-Meadow, who has written widely on mediation. See in particular C. Menkel-Meadow, 'The many ways of mediation: the transformation of tradition, ideologies, paradigms and practices', *Negotiation Journal*, 11 (1995), 217–42.

neutral expert fact-finding, med-arb and mini-trials.[3] With the exception of arbitration and mini-trials, most forms of ADR are species of facilitated settlement. These processes are called 'alternative' because they are ways of resolving disputes that theoretically do not require the involvement of any aspect of the legal system and because the approach to achieving settlement will not depend on reference to legal rights or the legal merits of the dispute, but will approach the dispute as a problem capable of solution. The eventual settlement can incorporate anything to which the parties will agree and does not have to bear any relationship either to the type or to the magnitude of any remedy that would have been available under the law. Indeed the 'spirit' of mediation is precisely to shift away from a focus on legal entitlement to a problem-solving frame of reference. It is about different interests and seeking to achieve a settlement that maximises the opportunities for both sides to achieve their interests.

A critical feature of all forms of ADR is that they are dispute resolution processes conducted in private. Both the process and outcome of the procedures are private and generally confidential to the parties. Like other types of out-of-court settlement, the terms of mediated agreements are not publicly known.

Despite the range of processes included under the ADR umbrella or within the ADR tent, in common with much of the current ADR policy, in these lectures I am generally

---

[3] For a discussion of these various processes see, Karl Mackie, David Miles, William Marsh and Tony Allen, *The ADR Practice Guide: Commercial Dispute Resolution*, 3rd revised edn (Tottel Publishing, 2007), Chapter 3.

referring to mediation rather than to other forms of private dispute resolution. The basic definition of mediation is that of a voluntary process in which a neutral third party assists disputing parties to reach a consensual solution to their dispute. This characteristic distinguishes mediation from partisan negotiations carried out between lawyers on behalf of their clients. In classic 'facilitative' mediation, the mediator has no authority to impose a solution on the parties and the aim of the mediation is to achieve a settlement, or at least a clarification of the issues in dispute. Mediation is distinguished from litigation processes by virtue of its focus on problem solving, rather than an emphasis on strict legal rights. Mediation is often said to be capable of producing 'win/win' situations rather than the 'win/ lose' situations characteristic of court adjudication. Mediation is said to be better than litigation for the resolution of non-family civil disputes because it is cheaper and quicker; because it is a flexible procedure that can achieve settlement in a wide range of disputes; that it is capable of achieving creative solutions that would not be available in court adjudication; that it focuses on commercial realities of disputes rather than legal technicalities; that it can repair damaged relationships; that it can reduce conflict; and that it is less stressful for parties than court procedures.

The use of the word 'alternative' in pro-mediation discourse tends to be interpreted as alternative to litigation and adjudication. This is somewhat deceptive since although the benefits of mediation are generally set in opposition to adjudication, in civil cases at least, the most common form of conclusion to litigation is an out-of-court settlement, rather than adjudication. A very high proportion of civil disputes

ADR AND CIVIL JUSTICE

commenced in the courts conclude on the basis of an out-of-court settlement and this was the modal pattern in English civil litigation throughout the twentieth century – especially so over the past twenty years, as discussed in the previous chapter.

The promise of mediation

The mediation literature is characterised by an interesting divergence, if not polarisation, of view. This seems to occur because, as Carrie Menkel-Meadow has pointed out, mediation is both an ideology (almost a religion) and a practice. The ideology is of peace seeking, transformative conflict resolving and human problem solving. The practice is of task-oriented, communication-enhancing dispute settlement. This leads to controversies about its appropriate definitions, forms and boundaries.[4]

In my experience, both the ideology and practice of mediation can encourage a zealot-like adherence among recent converts – perhaps people weary of adversarialism. New recruits to mediation often appear as shiny-eyed evangelists for whom litigation and adjudication are horrors not to be contemplated, while mediation offers a nirvana-like vision of a world rid of conflict, with only peace. For passionate adherents, there is no value in judicial determination; there are no legal rights, only clashing interests and problems to be solved. Although Menkel-Meadow is one of the more balanced commentators, who see a

[4] C. Menkel-Meadow (ed.), *Mediation: Theory, Policy and Practice* (Ashgate, 2001), Introduction, p. xvii.

role for adjudication in certain kinds of cases,[5] she has argued persuasively that the time for adversarialism and adjudication is over. She suggests that 'if late twentieth century learning has taught us anything, it is that truth is illusive, partial, interpretable, dependent on the characteristics of the knowers as well as the known, and, most importantly, complex.'[6] She suggests that courts with their 'limited remedial imaginations' may not be the best institutional settings for resolving some of the disputes that are put to them. Her argument expresses a postmodernist scepticism about facts and interpretation of facts, to which I will return later. She says that the legacy of postmodernism is that truth is not fixed, meanings are located provisionally, not discovered, and people who find truth, whether judges, juries, critics or even scientists, have interests – social, economic, political, racial, gender – that affect how they see the world. She argues that if we believe any of this, then we must inevitably question how the legal system can, with confidence, assess truth, assign liability and impose penalties. According to this view, authoritative determination appears inappropriate whereas mediation is capable of dealing with uncertainties and relativities.

On the other side, the proponents of judicial determination, those who have been referred to as 'adjudication romantics',[7]

---

[5] C. Menkel-Meadow, 'Whose dispute is it anyway?: A philosophical and democratic defense of settlement (in some cases)', *Georgetown Law Journal*, 83 (1995), 2663–96.

[6] C. Menkel-Meadow, 'The trouble with the adversary system in a postmodern, multicultural world', *William and Mary Law Review*, 38 (1996), 5–44, 5.

[7] Judith Resnik, Marc Galanter and David Luban are prominent and compelling examples. See also D.R. Hensler, 'Suppose it's not true: challenging mediation ideology', *Journal of Dispute Resolution*, (2002), 81–100.

draw attention to adjudication as a critical social practice that resolves disputes, defines and refines the law, reinforces important public values and is itself a defining democratic ritual that works the law 'pure'.[8] A crucial feature of adjudication is its public nature. Judith Resnik, who does not, in fact, regard herself as an adjudication 'romantic', has argued that adjudication is about more than the opportunity to debate conflicting rights claims; that it is itself a democratic practice which momentarily equalises power between individuals and between the individual and the State:

> [Adjudication is] itself a democratic practice – an odd moment in which individuals can oblige others to treat them as equals as they argue – in public – about alleged misbehaviour and wrongdoing.[9]

Moreover, advocates of adjudication do not see resort to the courts as necessarily negative. It has been argued that participation in litigation 'involves an affirmation of community', a willingness to subject oneself to the community's standards and procedures and cede a degree of autonomy in the interest of community cohesion. If participation

---

[8] D. Luban, 'Settlements and the erosion of the public realm', *Georgetown Law Journal* 83 (1994–5), 2619–62. 'Instead of treating adjudication as a social service that the state provides disputing parties to keep the peace, the public life conception treats disputing parties as … an occasion for the law to work itself pure … the litigants serve as nerve endings registering the aches and pains of the body politic, which the court attempts to treat by refining the law. Using litigants as stimuli for refining the law is a legitimate public interest in the literal sense … The law is a self-portrait of our politics, and adjudication is at once the interpretation and the refinement of the portrait', p. 2638.

[9] J. Resnik, 'Courts: in and out of sight, site and cite', *Villanova Law Review*, 53 (2008), 771–810, 806.

in community activities is an important barometer of national health, then the opportunity to participate in a public, legally binding dispute resolution process is an important measure of the health of our democracy.[10]

Thus the proponents of mediation are anti-adjudication and anti-litigation and the proponents of adjudication are 'against settlement'. The ultimate exemplar of the pro-adjudication/anti-settlement camp is Owen Fiss's seminal article 'Against settlement', which argues that ADR trivialises the value of lawsuits and reduces the social function of adjudication to the narrow purpose of resolving private disputes.[11] But, as discussed in Chapter 1, Fiss points out that adjudication is by judges who, like members of the legislative and executive branches, possess a power that has been defined and conferred by public law, not by private agreement. Their job is not simply to secure the peace but to explicate and give force to the values embodied in the law.

The philosophy of mediation

Cutting across these rather polarised views of mediation are what Baruch Bush and Folger describe as four different 'stories' about mediation and its goals.[12] They argue that while these stories or accounts of mediation reflect divergent

---

[10] R.M. Ackerman, 'Vanishing trial, vanishing community? The potential effect of the vanishing trial on America's social capital', *Journal of Dispute Resolution*, 7 (2006), 165–181, 166.

[11] O. Fiss, 'Against settlement', *Yale Law Journal*, 93 (1983–84), 1073–92.

[12] R.A. Baruch Bush and J.P. Folger, *The Promise of Mediation: The Transformative Approach to Conflict* (Jossey-Bass, 2005), pp. 9–19.

views in the literature, an appreciation of them is necessary in order to understand both the philosophy of mediation and also some of the concerns about it as a substitute for judicial determination.

The first of these accounts of the value of mediation can be found in what Baruch Bush and Folger call the 'satisfaction' story. This description of mediation suggests that it is a powerful tool for 'satisfying human needs and reducing suffering for parties to individual disputes'. The critical characteristics of consensuality, flexibility and informality mean that mediation can reveal all aspects of the 'problem' facing the parties. Most importantly, because mediation is not limited by legal categories or rules 'it can help reframe a contentious dispute as a mutual problem'.[13] In this version mediation facilitates collaborative, integrative problem solving, rather than adversarial bargaining. It can therefore produce creative win/win outcomes that go beyond formal rights to solve problems and satisfy parties' needs or remedy a party's difficulties. The vision is of superior outcomes – something more and better than could be achieved by adjudication, although no contrast is made with ordinary settlement negotiations. In comparison with formal adversarial processes, mediation is characterised by informality that reduces the economic and emotional costs of dispute settlement, producing private savings for parties. By preventing cases from going to court, it is argued that mediation also saves public expense, frees up the courts for other disputes, reduces delay and increases access to justice. In short, in this version mediation is quick, cheap, less

[13] Ibid, p. 9.

stressful, more creative and capable of offering the possibility of reconciliation between disputing parties. But in establishing its benefits the touchstone is always trial – which is always set up as damaging and negative. There is no possibility of empowerment or self-realisation through securing judicial determination of rights – only misery. Baruch Bush and Folger suggest that while this version of the mediation story is told by practising mediators, it has also been promoted by influential academics, judges and other judicial opinion formers, some of whom are themselves mediators.[14]

A second and powerful 'story' about mediation is that which focuses on its transformative potential. According to the 'transformation' story, mediation has the unique capacity to 'transform the quality of conflict interaction itself, so that conflicts can actually strengthen both the parties and the society' of which they are part. Again the informality, flexibility and consensuality of mediation permits parties to define their disputes or 'problems' and goals in their own terms and helps them to mobilise their personal resources to tackle their problems and to achieve their goals. This helps people to gain a greater sense of self-respect, self-reliance and self-confidence.[15] This has been called the empowerment dimension of the mediation process. Moreover, because mediation is non-judgemental it allows people to explain themselves to one another, and this can offer what is deemed to be a 'humanising' process in situations of conflict. While Baruch Bush and Folger were principally responsible for formally expounding this theory of mediation in the first

[14] Ibid, p. 11.
[15] Ibid, p. 13.

edition of their book in 1994, they suggest that before that time the transformative potential of mediation was recognised by academics and mediation practitioners and was, in their words, 'the underground story of the movement, often the motivating force behind practitioners' involvement'.[16]

A third analysis of the value of mediation is what Baruch Bush and Folger call the 'social justice' story. This tells us that mediation also 'offers an effective means of organizing individuals around common interests and thereby building stronger community ties and structures'. The capacity of mediation to 'reframe issues' and focus on common interest means that those involved in disputes who initially see themselves as adversaries can be assisted to appreciate a 'larger context' and to see that, perhaps, the disputants face a common enemy. So, for example, in neighbourhood mediation tenants might be helped to see that rather than focusing on their grievance with a neighbour, they in fact have a larger interest in common with their neighbour and against their landlord. The potential of mediation to achieve this kind of 'social justice' outcome is most often promoted by scholars and commentators involved with grassroots community organisations.[17]

While these three accounts of mediation point to its positive effects or potential, Baruch Bush and Folger set out another 'story' which represents a warning and which highlights the negative potential of mediation – what they refer to as the 'oppression story'. According to these analyses, whatever the original intentions of those who developed the field,

[16] Ibid, p. 15.
[17] Ibid, pp. 12–13.

mediation has turned out to be dangerous. Critics argue that it increases the power of the strong over the weak. Precisely because it is an informal and consensual process it can be used as an inexpensive and expedient adjunct to formal legal processes seeming to increase access to justice, whereas in fact it can magnify power imbalances and open the door to coercion and manipulation by the stronger party. At the same time it is argued that the posture of neutrality relieves the mediator of responsibility for preventing this.[18] As a result, mediation outcomes are unjust, favouring the stronger party. Such criticisms have been levelled at the movement as a whole,[19] at the inherent dangers it can present for equal opportunities,[20]

[18] See L. Mulcahy, 'The possibilities and desirability of mediator neutrality – towards an ethics of partiality?', *Social & Legal Studies*, 10:4 (2001), 505–27 (arguing that mediator neutrality may work to the disadvantage of weaker parties in mediation).

[19] For example R.L. Abel, 'The contradictions of informal justice' in R.L. Abel (ed.), *The Politics of Informal Justice, Volume 1: The American Experience* (Academic Press, 1982).

[20] The classic criticism can be found in Richard Delgado et al., 'Fairness and formality: minimizing the risk of prejudice in alternative dispute resolution', *Wisconsin Law Review* (1985), 1359 (arguing that ADR increases the risk of prejudice towards vulnerable disputants. A review of social science writings on prejudice reveals that the rules and structures of formal justice tend to suppress bias, whereas informality tends to increase it). For more recent research that supports these concerns see P.E. Bernard, 'Minorities, mediation and method: the view from one court-connected mediation program', *Fordham Urban Law Journal*, January, 35 (2008), 1. Bernard concludes in relation to small-claims mediation: 'The alternative dispute resolution ("ADR") field has awakened to the fact that the standard model of mediation assumes a balance of power between the parties, and that this is a false assumption in most small claims court cases, particularly in urban areas. If a court-connected mediation program seeks to be a vehicle for justice,

and in the field of family mediation, the dangers presented for women.[21] Divorce mediation is said to remove the safeguards that women would experience with partial representation in court proceedings.[22] As Baruch Bush and Folger admit, most writers and thinkers concerned with equality tend to raise such objections to mediation.

These different evaluations of the benefits and dangers of mediation reflect the diversity of conflicts that require resolution or determination and the different approaches and goals of mediation. The stories about what mediation might be trying to achieve or what it might have to offer underline the difficulty of generalising about the relevance, application and possible benefits of mediation. What you might hope to accomplish in the fraught and fractious context of family mediation where heartbreaking struggles occur over, for example, how often and when a child will spend time with a parent, is different from the kind of relationship tussle that may take place in the context of a commercial partnership breakdown. It is also different from what one might need and hope to accomplish in a dispute between warring neighbours. But it is also very different from what one might need and hope to accomplish in a dispute between a house owner and a builder who has wrecked the kitchen, where there is no desire for the relationship to

it must consider power imbalance not only in terms of racial or ethnic demographics, but particularly in terms of socio-economic class.'

[21] T. Grillo, 'The mediation alternative: process dangers for women', *Yale Law Journal*, 100:6 (1991), 1545–610.

[22] J. Eekelaar, 'Family justice: ideal or illusion? Family law and communitarian values' in M.D.A. Freeman (ed.), *Current Legal Problems* (Oxford University Press, 1996), pp. 161–216.

continue. All that the house owner wants is compensation, to get the problem fixed and to get on with her life. As Deborah Hensler has noted, the caseloads of most courts are not characterised by large numbers of public policy disputes or disputes between people in close personal relationships. 'Civil calendars do contain large numbers of disputes between strangers (e.g. victims and perpetrators of accidents) and other people whose relationships are not intimate (e.g. employers and employees, business firms and consumers) … where the traditional remedy is monetary compensation. It is this expansion of court-mandated mediation that appears to be responsible for reshaping how judges view the role of the courts.'[23]

ADR policy in England since 1995

Focusing on the potential of mediation to resolve non-family civil and commercial disputes, I want now to consider developments in mediation policy in England since the mid-1990s. Although arbitration and conciliation have a relatively long history in the development of alternatives to court for civil and commercial disputes,[24] the contemporary history of civil mediation in England effectively starts in the early 1990s and probably with the establishment of the Centre for Effective Dispute Resolution (CEDR) in London in 1990. Prior to the publication of Lord Woolf's 1995 *Interim Report*, mediation providers had been working hard to promote the value of mediation and other ADR processes as the answer to the

---

[23] D.R. Hensler, 'Suppose it's not true: challenging mediation ideology', 82.
[24] H. Brown and A. Marriott, *ADR Principles and Practice*, 2nd edn (Sweet & Maxwell, 1999), pp. 49–60.

perceived problems of civil justice. This campaign had only limited success, even in the realm of commercial disputes, until Lord Woolf gave mediation his stamp of approval in the reforms to civil justice in 1996.

The 1995 *Interim Report* on *Access to Justice* constituted a watershed in the development of ADR in England for civil and commercial disputes. As discussed in the previous chapter, a fundamental premise of the report was that court proceedings should be issued as a last resort, that all cases should be settled as soon as possible and that ADR should be tried before and after the issue of court proceedings in order to achieve early settlement. While the 1995 *Interim Report* provided encouragement for litigants to consider using ADR, the tone was more directive in the 1996 *Final Report.*

Lord Woolf promoted ADR because in his view it had the advantage of saving scarce judicial resources and because it offered benefits to litigants or potential litigants by being cheaper than litigation and producing quicker results.[25] In the 1995 *Interim Report*, Lord Woolf stated that the courts had an important role in providing information about ADR and encouraging its use in appropriate cases. This encouragement was strengthened in the 1996 *Final Report*,[26] which stated that:

> [T]he court will encourage the use of ADR at case
> management conferences and pre-trial reviews, and will
> take into account whether the parties have unreasonably

[25] The Rt Hon. Lord Woolf, *Access to Justice, Interim Report* (Lord Chancellor's Department, 1995), Chapter 18.

[26] The Rt Hon. Lord Woolf, *Final Report to the Lord Chancellor on the Civil Justice System in England and Wales* (HMSO, July 1996).

refused to try ADR or behaved unreasonably in the course of ADR.

The *Final Report* declared that the new landscape would have a number of features. These were that litigation will be avoided wherever possible; people will be encouraged to start court proceedings to resolve disputes only as a last resort, and after using other more appropriate means when these are available; information on sources of ADR will be provided at all civil courts; and legal aid funding will be available for pre-litigation resolution and ADR. The new landscape of civil justice would also have the feature that litigation will be less adversarial and more co-operative and that the court will encourage the use of ADR at case-management conferences and pre-trial reviews.

The strength of Lord Woolf's conviction that the public should be trying mediation rather than litigation was given expression in the Civil Procedure Rules, which conferred on the court the authority to order parties to attempt to settle their case using ADR and the judge the power to deprive a party of their legal costs if, in the court's view, the party has behaved unreasonably during the course of the litigation.[27] [28] This discretion is of considerable significance when legal costs

---

[27] CPR R1.4 (2) and CPR R26.4: stay of proceedings for settlement at the court's instigation. Factors to be taken into account when deciding costs issues include 'the efforts made, if any before and during the proceedings in order to try and resolve the dispute' (Parts 1 and 44, Civil Procedure Rules).

[28] In deciding what order (if any) to make about costs, the court must have regard to all the circumstances, including the conduct of the parties before and during the proceedings.

are often equal to, and may dwarf, the amount of money at stake in the dispute. The effect of the rules in relation to ADR is not to provide a direct incentive for parties to settle disputes by mediation but to impose a future threat of financial penalty on a party who might be deemed to have unreasonably refused an offer of mediation.

The emphasis on ADR in court rules was reinforced by the publication of eight pre-action protocols,[29] each of which encourages parties to attempt to settle their dispute, including by consideration of ADR, before beginning court proceedings. The most recent update of the Civil Procedure Rules includes the requirement that parties to any dispute should follow a reasonable pre-action procedure intended to avoid litigation, before making any application to the court. This should include negotiations with a view to settling the claim and, again, cost penalties can be applied to those who do not comply.

Although Lord Woolf did not propose that ADR should be compulsory before or after the issue of proceedings, the inclusion in the Civil Procedure Rules of a judicial power to direct the parties to attempt ADR, coupled with the court's discretion to impose a costs penalty on those who behave unreasonably during the course of litigation, has created a situation in which parties may feel that they have no choice.[30]

---

[29] Protocols lay down guidance for the parties on action to be taken for particular kinds of claim. They deal with attempts to settle the dispute and disclosure of documents.

[30] CPR R26.4 and Part 44 costs discretion. 'The court will encourage the use of ADR at case management conferences and pre-trial reviews, and will take into account whether the parties have unreasonably refused to try ADR.'

It is worth pausing for a moment to consider the underlying messages of the *Access to Justice* report and why ADR was being promoted so vigorously. The message being communicated was that seeking justice through public, state-sponsored dispute resolution processes (i.e. the courts) is inevitably time-consuming, stressful, unpredictable and expensive. It is therefore better to seek to resolve disputes by mediation, which is a private dispute resolution process. The premises underlying this argument, however, seem to be as follows. First, access to the courts is difficult for most people; there are no public funds for ordinary citizens to seek to protect their rights or enforce the obligations of others, or to make good their entitlements. Second, it is impossible to make the process much quicker or judicial determination any less unpleasant. Third, in any case, the outcome is always unpredictable if not capricious. Fourth, disputes are at bottom a clash of interests which do not justify the imposition of judicial authority and can generally be settled. Finally, sensible people do not want to litigate.

There is also an interesting question about the types of cases for which scarce judicial resources were being conserved. If the motivation was to save the judiciary for high-value, interesting commercial cases, then they would be competing for the same work as the mediators whose services were being promoted. While mediators may be committed to fostering harmony and reducing conflict in society, they are not uninterested in the profits to be made from assisting with large commercial disputes. Indeed, with encouragement from mediators, the judges in the Commercial Court in London have since 1993, through a series of Practice Statements, been directing selected cases to attempt to settle by means of an ADR procedure.[31]

Lord Woolf's enthusiasm for ADR was infectious among some sections of the judiciary. Judges started to train as mediators and in county courts around the country sought permission to establish mediation schemes within their courts. The government happily provided the resources for these schemes to be established. In the late 1990s and early 2000s, mediation schemes were set up in Central London, Exeter and Bristol and these later spread to Birmingham, Manchester, Guildford, Reading and elsewhere.[32] These special schemes offered no or low-cost, time-limited mediation for litigants who had already commenced court proceedings. It was an opportunity to come to the court for a three-hour mediation to see whether the case could be settled. Mediation was provided by trained mediators, usually on

[31] For an evaluation of the operation of Commercial Court ADR Orders see H. Genn, *Court Based ADR Initiatives for Non-Family Civil Cases* (Department for Constitutional Affairs, Research series 1/02, 2002).

[32] M. Doyle, *Manchester Small Claims Mediation Scheme Evaluation* (Department for Constitutional Affairs, 2006); J. Enterken and M. Sefton, *Evaluation of Reading Small Claims Mediation Scheme* (Department for Constitutional Affairs, 2006); S. Prince, *Evaluation of Exeter Small Claims Mediation Scheme* (Department for Constitutional Affairs, 2006); S. Prince and S. Belcher, *An Evaluation of the Effectiveness of Court-based Mediation Processes in Non-Family Civil Proceedings at Exeter and Guildford County Courts* (Department for Constitutional Affairs, 2006); L. Webley, P. Abrams and S. Bacquet, *Evaluation of Birmingham Fast and Multi Track Mediation Scheme* (Department for Constitutional Affairs, 2006); H. Genn, *Central London Pilot Mediation Scheme, Evaluation Report* (Department for Constitutional Affairs, 1998).

a pro-bono basis. There was no shortage of mediators. The mediation provider organisations had been nudging both the judiciary and policy makers behind the scenes and were more than happy to co-operate with court-annexed mediation schemes by offering the services of trained mediators for no fee. They were content to do this because it provided work for trained mediators keen to try out their newly acquired skills.

However, despite the enthusiasm for mediation shown by some sections of the judiciary, the voluntary uptake in these court schemes between 1996 and 2001 remained stubbornly low. There was no wholesale rush to mediation. No Damascene Conversion. The courts kept encouraging litigants to mediate, but litigants mulishly ignored or rejected those offers. It was therefore time for judicial action. Beginning in 2002, a series of landmark decisions was handed down from the Court of Appeal and High Court underlining the importance of ADR. In *Cowl*[33] in 2002 Lord Woolf held that parties must consider ADR before starting legal proceedings, particularly where public money was involved. This was followed more significantly by *Dunnett v Railtrack*[34] in which the court dismissed Mrs Dunnett's appeal against Railtrack, but nonetheless refused to order Mrs Dunnett to pay Railtrack's costs in the appeal. Applying Part 44 of the CPR and taking into account the overriding objective of the CPR to deal with cases 'justly', the court decided that Railtrack's refusal to contemplate mediation prior to the appeal (after it had been suggested

---

[33] *Cowl and Others v Plymouth City Council* [2001] EWCA Civ 1935.
[34] *Dunnett v Railtrack plc* [2002] EWCA Civ 2003.

by the court) was sufficient, in the court's view, to deny the company its legal costs.

The message of *Dunnett v Railtrack* was reinforced in the later case of *Hurst v Leeming*[35] in which Mr Justice Lightman held that it is for the judge to decide whether a refusal to mediate was justified. In a frequently repeated statement the judge argued that 'mediation is not in law compulsory, but alternative dispute resolution is at the heart of today's civil justice system'. He went on to threaten that an unjustified failure to consider mediation would attract adverse consequences. While judges will accept valid reasons for not wanting to proceed with ADR, such reasons must be fully justifiable if the party wishes to avoid being penalised by the court. A further case in 2003 confirmed the risks for parties if they unreasonably refused to try ADR or withdrew unreasonably from an ADR process.[36] However, the high-water mark in the line of cases came in May 2003 when the High Court made another significant decision in relation to the use of ADR. The case of *Royal Bank of Canada Trust Corporation Ltd v Secretary of State for Defence* centred on a point of law relating to a lease.[37] The claimant was willing to try to resolve the dispute by ADR, but the Ministry of Defence rejected the suggestion on the ground that the dispute involved a point of law that required a 'black and white' answer. In the High Court, the Department

---

[35] [2001] EWHC 1051 Ch, but judgment given on 9 May 2002 after the *Dunnett* decision.
[36] *Leicester Circuits Ltd v Coates Brothers Plc* [2003] EWCA Civ 290 – withdrawal from mediation is contrary to the spirit of the Civil Procedure Rules (March 2003).
[37] [2003] EWHC 1479 (Ch).

was successful on the point of law, but the judge refused to award the Department its legal costs as a result of its refusal to mediate. The judge stated that the reason given for refusing mediation (i.e. that the case involved a point of law) did not make the case unsuitable. Mediation providers greeted this decision with considerable satisfaction.[38]

By mid-2003, the courts had indicated clearly that refusing an offer of mediation carried with it a significant danger that costs might be denied to the refusing party, even when they had been successful in the litigation. But in 2004, the tide appeared to turn somewhat in the Court of Appeal case of *Halsey v Milton Keynes General NHS Trust*.[39] The case again concerned the question of when the court might impose a costs penalty following a refusal to attempt mediation. The case had been the subject of discussion for some time before the judgment was issued because the court, unusually, had requested opinions from the Civil Mediation Council, the ADR Group and CEDR (two of the largest commercial mediation providers) about the value of mediation. The Law Society had also submitted an opinion. In its judgment, which sought to lay down guidelines for the courts in dealing with costs in situations where mediation has been refused, the Court of Appeal did not accept the Civil Mediation

---

[38] CEDR, the leading commercial mediation provider organisation, commenting on the decision said that it 'follows in a direct line from *Dunnett* v. *Railtrack*, *Hurst* v. *Leeming* and *Leicester Circuits* v. *Coates Industries*, providing further examples of failed arguments to avoid mediation. More specifically, the case makes it clear that it is dangerous for a government party to ignore its own public undertaking to use ADR'. CEDR, 'Public sector – a culture change?', *Resolutions*, 23 (Summer 2003), 6, www.cedr.co.uk/news/resolutions/resolutions32.pdf

[39] [2004] EWCA (Civ) 576.

Council's argument that there should be a general presumption in favour of mediation, but instead accepted the submission of the Law Society that the question of whether mediation had been 'unreasonably' refused should depend on a number of factors, which should be evaluated by the court in each case. In laying down guidelines for the courts, the Court of Appeal held that there was no general presumption in favour of mediation. Most importantly, Lord Justice Dyson significantly and evidently deliberately held that the courts have no power to *order* mediation and in this context raised the question of whether a court order to mediate might infringe Article 6 of the Human Rights Act 1998. He also concluded that although the court has jurisdiction to impose a costs sanction on successful parties who unreasonably decline to mediate, in deciding whether or not to do so factors to consider include whether the successful party reasonably believed they would win, cost–benefit and whether the unsuccessful party can show that mediation had a reasonable prospect of success.

Halsey attempted to turn back the tide, the decision having been given by a judicial ADR non-believer or at least a judicial ADR sceptic. The decision threw the mediation providers into disarray and led to much scratching of brows.[40] However, there appears to have been a subsequent campaign, launched at the highest judicial level, to undermine the

---

[40] P. Hughes, 'When will the courts penalise refusal of mediation? New Court of Appeal guidance' (Crutes Law Firm, 2004) www.crutes.co.uk/content/news/archives04/willcourtspenaliserefusalofmediation.asp; T. Allen, 'A closer look at *Halsey* and Steel', CEDR, June 2004, www.cedr.com/index.php?location=/library/articles/A_closer_look_at_Halsey_and_Steel.htm

authority of Lord Justice Dyson's decision in *Halsey*. In a speech in India in March 2008, the previous Lord Chief Justice, Lord Phillips, said that the *Halsey* decision had reduced the pressure on English litigants to attempt mediation. He confessed that although at the time of Lord Justice Dyson's judgment he had agreed with it, he had now had second thoughts. He said: 'With hindsight I tend to agree [with a criticism made of the case by Mr Justice Lightman] that it is a pity that he said what he did about burden of proof. There is much to be said for the robust attitude that a party who refuses to attempt mediation should have to justify his refusal.'[41] This was followed fairly rapidly by a speech by the Master of the Rolls and Head of Civil Justice, Lord Justice Clarke, to a mediation conference in Birmingham in May 2008. In this speech he attacked Lord Justice Dyson's assertion that an order for ADR might breach Article 6 of the HRA. He said that in his view compulsory ADR does not violate Article 6 and so there may be grounds for suggesting that *Halsey* was wrong on the Article 6 point.[42] He concluded that

---

[41] Lord Phillips of Worth Matravers, Lord Chief Justice, 'Alternative dispute resolution: an English viewpoint', Speech, India, 29 March 2008, www.judiciary.gov.uk/docs/speeches/lcj_adr_india_290308.pdf

[42] 'Taken together, what could be described as the European and US approach to ADR appears to demonstrate that compulsory ADR does not in and of itself give rise to a violation of Article 6 or of the equivalent US constitutional right of due process. This suggests, admittedly without hearing argument, that the *Halsey* approach may have been overly cautious. The issue before the court then was "when should a court impose costs sanctions against a successful litigant on the grounds that he has refused to take part in an alternative dispute resolution ('ADR')?". Whatever the Court of Appeal held in *Halsey* in answer to that question, its comments regarding compulsory ADR were surely what we used to call *obiter dicta*, although I note that they

the courts retain a jurisdiction to require parties to enter into mediation. While this latter view must surely be correct, what is interesting is that care has been taken to publicise that view. Indeed, the speeches were evidently orchestrated in order to rob *Halsey* of its authority – in effect to return thinking back to the pre-*Halsey* approach.

Government policy on ADR in civil justice

Although government policy on ADR over the last decade in England has rather lagged behind judicial enthusiasm and activism, the steps taken to promote the use of ADR must be seen in the context of increasing expenditure on criminal justice and the need to control expenditure on civil legal aid and the civil courts. In its landmark White Paper, *Modernising Justice*, published in 1998, the government made clear that it was seeking to improve the range of options available for dispute resolution and that it would consider the contribution that ADR could make to the civil justice system, including mediation, arbitration and ombudsman schemes. However, aside from speeches from the Lord Chancellor, one or two discussion papers and facilitation of court-annexed mediation schemes, few significant measures were introduced until

have subsequently been summarised in, for instance, *Hickman v Blake Lapthorn* [2006] EWHC 12 (QB) as establishing that compulsory ADR is contrary to Article 6 ECHR. But again that summary contained no more than *obiter dicta*. With that in mind it seems to me at any rate that despite the *Halsey* decision it is at least strongly arguable that the court retains a jurisdiction to require parties to enter into mediation.' Annual Mediation Council Conference, Birmingham (May 2008), www. judiciary.gov.uk/docs/speeches/mr_mediation_conference_may08.pdf the Access to Justice Act 1999, when the changes to the legal aid system offered the government an opportunity to manifest its commitment to supporting the growth of ADR. Under the 1999 Act, the Community Legal Service Fund (administered by the Legal Services Commission) replaced the old legal aid scheme and introduced a new set of rules governing eligibility for legal aid support. The rules (contained in the Funding Code and Funding Code Guidance)[43] include the cost of mediation within the legal aid system and a condition that an application for legal aid for representation may be refused if there are ADR options that ought to be tried first. In 2004 the Legal Services Commission published a consultation paper, the title of which is worth giving in full: 'A new focus for civil legal aid: Encouraging early resolution and discouraging unnecessary litigation.' The paper invited comments on proposals to 're-prioritise' legal aid funding 'so that early and effective dispute resolution is encouraged and unnecessary litigation is discouraged'. The result is increased pressure on those applying for legal aid to attempt mediation. The most recent version of the Legal Services Commission's funding code, published in June 2005, indicates that 'an application for funding may be refused if there are complaint systems, ombudsman schemes or forms of alternative dispute resolution which should be tried before litigation is pursued'.[44] In essence, this means that citizens hoping for public funding for representation in non-family civil actions must have attempted mediation or be able to show why it was not possible to do so.

[43] December 2003, R11.
[44] Criterion 5.4.3.

The Alternative Dispute Resolution section of the 2005 Funding Code Decision-Making Guidance states that 'all forms of ADR are accepted to have at least equal validity to court proceedings' and that ADR has received 'increased emphasis in the Community Legal Service'. As a result, decisions about legal aid may be contingent on willingness to enter mediation and the Code contains guidance on when the availability of ADR should lead 'to the refusal or suspension of Legal Representation'.[45] The Code states that non-family mediation is always a voluntary process 'in the sense that a mediator cannot impose a settlement on the parties', but regrets the fact that the purely voluntary nature of mediation has resulted in a 'surprisingly low take-up' from most organised mediation schemes. It contains a clear preference for mandatory mediation:

> Most solicitors or clients who are considering or are engaged in litigation seem to prefer to continue litigating rather than attempting mediation. The Commission believes that it is in the interests of clients for more non-family cases to attempt mediation and that some solicitors or clients will not properly consider mediation unless required to do so.[46]

From 2001 onwards, the DCA's explicit strategy was to reduce the proportion of disputes resolved by resort to the civil courts. The 2004–9 strategy included a target to reduce civil court hearings by 5 per cent by March 2008, despite the fact that

[45] *Funding Code Guidance Amendments: 'A New Focus For Civil Legal Aid'. Non-Family Guidance*, Part 7, Alternative Dispute Resolution (Legal Services Commission, 2005).
[46] Ibid, S7.6(6).

trial rates in the High Court and county courts (other than small claims) had already plunged. The key instrument for achieving this target was the encouragement, both in and outside the court structure, of the use of ADR. But how was this to be achieved? The DCA was already supporting court-annexed mediation schemes around the country with only very modest uptake – nothing that could produce the 5 per cent desired reduction. One possibility, apparently, was experimenting with compulsion.

Mandatory mediation has always been a controversial subject that promotes strong feelings and more than a little confusion in mediation rhetoric. The purist definition of mediation is that of a *voluntary, consensual* process in which the parties are assisted to reach settlement. Although Lord Woolf had explicitly set his face against making mediation compulsory, mediation practitioners and other mediation enthusiasts did not necessarily share Lord Woolf's concerns. Although accepting that at first sight the concept of mandatory mediation appears contradictory, frustration at the low voluntary uptake in the early 2000s, and concern about the number of trained mediators without work, led mediation providers to press for a more radical approach. Arguments were made to the DCA (including via the Civil Justice Council) that an experimental compulsory mediation scheme should be set up. The justification for such a step was that even if disputing parties were forced against their will to undergo a mediation experience, the attractions of the process would overcome resistance and the parties would be likely to settle. Moreover, compulsion would rapidly expose a large number of people to the positive experience of mediation, thus leading to the kind of 'take-off' that had to date been elusive.

The publication in March 2001 of the results of a large mandatory mediation programme for civil disputes in Canada gave some credence to this argument. It seemed that even though parties had been compelled to mediate, the results were positive. A systematic evaluation commissioned by the Ontario government concluded that mandatory mediation had speeded up cases, reduced costs to litigants, led to early settlements and resulted in litigant and lawyer satisfaction.[47] Encouraged by these results the DCA decided to go ahead with its own experiment. In March 2004, it set up a one-year pilot in Central London County Court in which cases were automatically referred to mediation (ARM) and while it was possible for parties to object to the referral, any unreasonable refusal to mediate would lead to costs sanctions. At the launch of the pilot in April 2004, it was explained that although some people thought that mediation should be voluntary, others believed that 'ADR would never become part of the mainstream of our litigation/dispute-resolution culture unless courts were more actively involved in promoting the use of ADR'. It was said that only by running the experiment would it be possible to find out whether the arguments against compulsion were borne out or whether those in favour of mandatory mediation would be supported.[48]

Unfortunately, the launch of the scheme precisely coincided with Lord Justice Dyson's judgment in the *Halsey* case

[47] R.G. Hann and C. Baar, *Evaluation of the Ontario Mandatory Mediation Program (Rule 24.1): Final Report – The First 23 Months* (Ontario Ministry of the Attorney General, March 2001).

[48] For detail on the background to the scheme and a full evaluation of the ARM pilot see H. Genn et al., *Twisting Arms: Court Referred and Court*

which clearly said that the court had no power to compel parties to enter a mediation process. It is difficult to assess precisely what impact the *Halsey* judgment had on the behaviour of those who were automatically referred to mediation during the course of the pilot, but there can be little doubt that the judgment did not help. The result of the pilot was almost exactly the opposite of what happened in Canada. While the Canadians experienced only a handful of cases in which the parties opted out of the mandatory mediation scheme, in the ARM pilot about 80 per cent of those referred to mediation objected to the referral and following the *Halsey* judgment the court seemed to be uneasy about forcing people to mediate against their will. Indeed, it was a classic example of policies colliding. A decision that the pilot had been largely unsuccessful was effectively taken after the experience of the first six months, although the scheme was allowed to run its course for a full year before being abandoned. What is instructive, however, in the current context is the fact that despite the failure of the ARM pilot, the interest in mandatory mediation continues among mediators, the judiciary and the Ministry of Justice. The continuing pressure for mandatory mediation is discussed further below.

What has been learned about mediation in England?

Unusually, and very helpfully, the government has invested quite heavily in evaluating a number of court-based

Linked Mediation Under Judicial Pressure (Ministry of Justice Research Series 1/07, 2007).

mediation schemes.[49] As a result there is a significant body of
empirical evidence about the potential of mediation for resolving civil and commercial disputes. Most of these schemes
followed a similar design. They were low cost, time limited
(usually three hours) and held on court premises after the end
of the normal court day (4.30–7.30 pm).[50] Although the courts
administered the schemes, the mediations themselves were
undertaken by trained mediators.

First of all demand. All of the court-based schemes
have demonstrated weak 'bottom-up' demand. This is particularly so for cases involving personal injury where the
demand has been virtually non-existent. Since in most county
courts personal injury cases account for more than half of the
defended caseload, the failure to attract PI cases into mediation
has been significant. Yet the overwhelming majority of PI cases
settle without trial in any case. Although the value of mediation is generally compared with trial and adjudication, the
challenge for mediation policy since the mid-1990s has been
that it is seeking to encourage facilitated settlement in a system
in which settlement is in any case the norm. Since most cases
settle, mediation is principally offering accelerated settlement.
But if one effect of the Woolf reforms has been to increase pre-
action settlement, then those cases that go to court are likely
to be the most contentious and therefore the least likely to be
interested in mediation soon after the issue of proceedings.

[49] See the evaluation reports commissioned by the Department for
Constitutional Affairs cited above at n. 31, n. 32 and n. 48.
[50] Although limited to three-hour sessions, most of the schemes permitted
a second session if it was not possible to reach a settlement after three
hours and it was felt that with more time a settlement could be reached.

Moreover, aside from sections of commercial practice, the profession is cautious about advising mediation and on the whole is not routinely recommending mediation. Although some might argue that this is because lawyers are mindful of their profits, it is also because they are still relatively unfamiliar with mediation. Lawyers responsible for the conduct of their cases find it difficult to envisage what value mediation might add to normal negotiation in a system that is in any case settlement dominated. Since most lawyers argue that their objective in litigation is to achieve a settlement rather than go to trial, many consider that they are already 'doing mediation' themselves. The same considerations may apply to parties. Many business people who find themselves in the middle of a dispute are experienced negotiators and understandably believe that if they have not been able to negotiate a settlement, then a mediator is unlikely to be able to assist.

It is also true that, in the early stages of a dispute at least, many litigants are not ready to mediate civil disputes. They are not ready to compromise, which is what mediation largely demands. There are different reasons for claimants and defendants. Claimants do not want to mediate because they take their lawyer's advice, because they want 'justice' not compromise, because they believe they will win and because they want their 'day in court'. So an early invitation to mediate may not sound particularly attractive – although the evidence is that claimants have been more likely to accept offers to mediate than defendants.

Defendants have different reasons for not wanting to mediate. There are broadly two types of defendant – those who do not want to pay and those who cannot pay. In the first

category are those who genuinely believe that they are not
liable and who hope that if they refuse to pay, the claimant
may become disheartened, exhausted or run out of money. In
the second category are those who are impecunious and who
are hoping that the case might collapse or who are simply put-
ting off the moment when they will be ordered to pay. For both
categories of defendant, delay is an advantage. So while the
message of quick, cheap resolution may be attractive to some
claimants, it is less so to the majority of defendants. Indeed,
defendants can be brought to the mediation table only by a
negative message – such as the threat of a financial penalty at
trial for failing to agree to mediate.

And what have we learned about motivation to mediate? Why do litigants accept the opportunity to mediate once
they have commenced court proceedings? It seems that the
principal motivation for mediating is to avoid the anticipated
cost, delay and discomfort of trial. It is not about reconciliation, or growth, or conflict reduction. It is because parties
have been told and believe that mediating is a quicker and
cheaper way of achieving some sort of remedy. More recently,
an important motivating factor seems to have been concern to
avoid the risk of *Dunnett v Railtrack*[51] cost penalties.

As far as customer satisfaction is concerned, evaluations of court-annexed mediation schemes show high levels of
satisfaction among those who *volunteer* to enter the process.
What parties value is the informality of the process and the
opportunity to be fully involved in the proceedings. They like
the lack of legal technicality and the opportunity to be heard

---

[51] [2002] EWCA Civ 2003.

at the beginning of the proceedings. Parties like the speed of the process and, among businesses, the focus on commercial issues in the case. However, they do not like being pressured to settle and some complain that they felt under such pressure.[52] The benefits of mediation are generally explained by comparison with the likely experience of the anticipated trial. This tendency to compare the experience with what might have happened at a trial is reinforced by the mediation process itself during which a principal tool for achieving settlement is to constantly remind parties of the 'danger' of not settling on the day and the unpleasantness that awaits them if they proceed through to trial.

On the question of speed and cost, analysis of large-scale data from court-based mediation schemes compared with control data provides no evidence to suggest any difference in case durations between mediated and non-mediated cases.[53] The same analysis does, however, show that time-limited mediation can avoid trials in non-PI cases, either through immediate settlement or through bringing the parties closer to settlement so that they can settle before trial.[54] The perceptions of mediators, parties and their lawyers is that successful mediation can save cost, but it is difficult to estimate how much, since, although the touchstone is always trial, the overwhelming majority of cases would not proceed to trial and would not therefore incur the costs of trial.[55] It is also clear, however, that unsuccessful mediation may *increase* the costs

[52] H. Genn et al., *Twisting Arms*, Chapters 3 and 5.
[53] H. Genn et al., *Twisting Arms*, p. 71.
[54] Ibid, p. 73.
[55] Ibid, p. 107.

for parties (estimated at between £1,500 and £2,000).[56] And this fact raises serious questions for policies that seek to pressure parties to enter mediation unwillingly.

Analyses of the outcome of mediation in these court-based schemes show that the readiness of parties to mediate is an important factor in settlement.[57] Put simply, cases are more likely to settle at mediation if the parties enter the process voluntarily rather than being pressured into the process. It seems clear that increased pressure to mediate depresses settlement rates. When people are forced to mediate, they may go through the motions without any intention of settling. They may use the opportunity to gain information about their opponent or to try to psyche out the opponent.

The other important lesson from mediation programmes for civil and commercial disputes is that most settlements involve simply a transfer of money. Only a small minority of settlements are in any way creative or provide something different from what would be available in court. It also seems clear that claimants significantly discount their claims in reaching mediated settlements.[58] There is a price to pay in terms of substantive justice for early settlement.

[56] Ibid, p. 110 and p. 183.
[57] This emerges from the findings of the ARM pilot and analyses of the voluntary mediation scheme at Central London County Court where the settlement rate declined from the high of 62% in 1998 to below 40% in 2000 and 2003. This interpretation for the falling settlement rate is supported by the views of mediators interviewed for that study, *Twisting Arms*, Chapter 6.
[58] H. Genn, *Central London Evaluation*, p. 71; L. Webley, *Birmingham Evaluation*, op. cit, pp. 70–71.

Mediation and access to justice

What, then, can we conclude about the contribution of mediation to access to justice? Many of the reforms to civil justice that have been implemented over the past few years argue that diverting legal disputes away from the courts and into mediation is, in fact, a strategy that will increase access to justice. But this is a claim that requires some unpacking. First, what do we mean by access to justice? The role of law and the rule of law are fundamental to liberal democracies which emphasise individualism and liberty and promise justice and equality before the law. Under the rule of law, law stands above all people and all people are equal before it. But for all people to be equal before the law there must be equal access to the law in order to make rights effective. In 1978 Sir Jack Jacob argued that access to justice is a profound social need:

> We must enable legal disputes, conflicts and complaints which inevitably arise in society to be resolved in an orderly way according to the justice of the case, so as to promote harmony and peace in society, lest they fester and breed discontent and disturbance.[59]

What is interesting about Sir Jack's statement is that in his vision, access to justice *promotes* peace and harmony in society. This vision is in sharp contrast with that of mediation

---

[59] Sir Jack Jacob, 'Access to justice in England' in M. Cappelletti and B. Garth (eds) *Access to Justice, Vol 1, A World Survey* (Milan, 1978), p. 417.

proponents who present justice and peace in opposition, rather than seeing peace flowing from justice.

It has been said that in practice access to justice defies definition. Certainly it is used as a handle to justify all sorts of policies designed to have quite different outcomes. At its most basic it is about access to procedures for making rights effective through state-sponsored public and fair dispute resolution processes. It implies equal access to authoritative enforceable rulings and outcomes that reflect the merits of the case in light of relevant legal principles. It does not imply that laws are necessarily just, but that individuals have a fair opportunity for their rights to be determined according to the prevailing promulgated rules. This conception of access to justice was used by Lord Justice Laws in the famous English case of *Witham*,[60] when he held, in the context of increased court fees, that access to the courts is a 'constitutional right' and made reference to the principle set out in Magna Carta: 'To no one will we sell, to no one will we refuse or delay, right or justice.'[61]

But much of the interest in ADR in jurisdictions around the world has grown out of a *failure* of the civil courts to provide access to fair procedures. In many parts of the world, both the criminal and civil courts are overloaded. In some places cases take years to be processed and concluded. Legal costs are often high and disproportionate. Enforcement is difficult. Some legal systems are corrupt. In many places there is little or no public funding for legal aid so little means of low-income groups obtaining quality legal representation.

[60] Mr Justice Laws, *Witham, R (on the application of) v Lord Chancellor* [1997] 2 All ER 779, at p. 787.
[61] *Magna Carta*, Clause 40 (1215).

ADR can be a means of citizens side-stepping legal systems in which the public have no confidence (especially for commercial disputes in newly independent states). More important, in such circumstances, the promotion of ADR by governments could be interpreted as less about the positive qualities of mediation and more about diverting cases to mediation as an easier and cheaper option than attempting to fix or invest in dysfunctional systems of adjudication. It is, in effect, a throwing up of hands – an admission of defeat.

As I argued in the previous chapter, in England the reform of civil justice arose not out of any sudden crisis in access to *civil* justice – or at least nothing that was particularly urgent or new at that moment in 1994 – but more as a result of the escalating costs of *criminal* justice within a single justice budget and the need to find savings from civil justice. Even though in 1999 the number of cases being issued in the civil courts was already declining, and despite the fact that civil legal aid was effectively abolished in the cutely named Access to Justice Act of the same year, there was still pressure to reduce expenditure on civil justice, and that pressure continues.

Policy makers may be interested in promoting ADR in order to clear court lists, reduce the legal aid bill, reduce enforcement problems, reduce court expenditure on judges or reduce expenditure on court administration. In which case, when it is asserted that mediation improves 'access to justice', what does that mean? Does mediation contribute to access to the courts? No, because it is specifically non-court based. Does it contribute to substantive justice? No, because mediation requires the parties to relinquish ideas of legal rights during mediation and focus, instead, on problem solving. Are mediators concerned about substantive justice? Absolutely not. That is the wrong question to ask. Mediation is about searching for a solution to a problem. There is no reference to the hypothesised outcome at trial. The mediator's role is to assist the parties in reaching a settlement of their dispute. The mediator does not make a judgement about the quality of the settlement. Success in mediation is a settlement that the parties can live with. The outcome of mediation is not about *just* settlement, it is *just about settlement*.

Although there is a 'justice-in-mediation' literature, it is clear that the concept of justice in mediation is different from justice in adjudication. As Hyman (2002) helpfully explains:

> Unlike a judge, jury or arbitrator, a mediator does not have the responsibility to determine an appropriate remedy or a just distribution. That is for parties themselves to do. The mediator must attend to the process, help the parties recognize the legitimacy of different perspectives on justice, and work towards a resolution that comports with the parties' considered views of a fair and acceptable outcome.[62]

We must therefore conclude that mediation may be about problem-solving, it may be about compromise, it may be about transformation and recognition, it may be about

---

[62] J.M. Hyman and L.P. Love, 'If Portia were a mediator: an inquiry into justice in mediation', *Clinical Law Review*, 9 (2002), 157, 159. See also Jacqueline M. Nolan-Haley, 'Court mediation and the search for justice through law', *Washington University Law Quarterly*, January (1996), 49. In explaining the role for justice in mediation she says: '[O]ur civil justice system has traditionally promised justice through law. The promise of mediation is different: Justice is derived, not through the operation of law, but through autonomy and self-determination.'

moral growth, it may be about communication, it may be about repairing damaged relationships – but it is not about substantive justice.[63] Concern for 'justice' and 'fairness' is not relevant to the goals of mediation.

If mediation does not increase access to the courts and does not increase access to substantive justice because the legal merits of cases are not relevant to the process of mediation, then what does it do? Carrie Menkel-Meadow provides an answer. As she has expressed it, the underlying goal of mediation in civil and commercial disputes is relatively modest. She suggests that mediation provides a responsive and individual solution to legal disputes which does 'no worse harm' to the parties than non-resolution of the dispute. We should not, therefore, be measuring the outcome of mediation in terms of access to justice or what the parties might have achieved via a well-functioning justice system. We should simply be measuring the outcome of mediation against doing nothing. That may be a perfectly acceptable objective, but if that represents the extent of the ambition for mediation, that should be made clear when discussing policy on diverting disputes away from court and into mediation. Essentially, expressed in terms of 'no worse harm', the access to justice contribution of mediation offers little more than closure of a dispute, however it is achieved. It would offer

---

[63] Some mediation proponents who worry about the justice-in-mediation issue argue that participants like mediation procedures and that their satisfaction with procedures leads to satisfaction with substantive outcome. Mediation offers procedural justice in that parties have an opportunity to tell their story, that they are listened to, treated with dignity and in an even-handed way. See for example, J.M. Hyman and L.P. Love, supra, pp. 157–194.

an access to justice benefit only for those who are currently taking *no* steps to achieve a resolution of their dispute. But those
now in the sights of government and judicial ADR policy are, in
fact, doing something. Claimants have already issued proceedings to achieve a resolution on the legal merits and at that point
may have a strong sense of a desire for justice.

> Parties who choose to bring their conflicts into the public
> domain of the court system are likely to have strong
> beliefs about their legal entitlements. For them, law may
> be an important, if not predominant, value. Otherwise,
> they might have resolved their disputes with less costly
> solutions, such as avoidance or a handshake.[64]

What mediation is offering is simply the opportunity to discount their claim in order to be spared the presumed misery
and uncertainty of the adjudication process. Indeed, the same
thing that ordinary settlement offers and the same inability to
imagine an adjudication process that could be less miserable.

The role of the judiciary in promoting ADR

A curious feature of the crises in civil justice and the
shift away from trials and adjudication has been the active part
that some sections of the judiciary in England, and in other
parts of the world, have played in supporting anti-litigation,
anti-adjudication rhetoric and the diversion of cases out of the
courts and into the hands of private dispute resolution. While
one might understand the hostility to civil justice of corporate

---

[64] J.M. Nolan-Haley, 'Court mediation and the search for justice through
law', pp. 64–5.

and institutional defendants and, indeed, governments, it is more difficult to comprehend the involvement in this trend by influential sections of the judiciary. What is the cause of a twenty-first-century loss of belief in the value of adjudication? Are the judiciary, as has been suggested by Judith Resnik, experiencing a postmodernist crisis in confidence in which there are no facts and there are no rules?

> [F]ederal judges begin to appear (oddly) aligned with movements denominated 'post-modern'. Federal judges may press for settlement because they themselves doubt their own capacities to find information sufficient to call 'fact' and are painfully aware of the plasticity of 'law'. Federal judges act as if they believe that stories dissolve in endless variations, none of which justify the imposition of state power. From this vantage point, federal judges can be understood as encouraging disputants to do as they want, for in these private accords lies as much – or as little – as what adjudication can offer.[65]

Has there been some loss of confidence in the judicial role? A loss of belief in the inherent value of their own authority? Or is it that after years on the other side of the bench, judges develop a distaste for adversarialism?[66] Have the judiciary been co-opted by the emerging profession of ADR providers? Or is

[65] J. Resnik, 'Trial as error, jurisdiction as injury: transforming the meaning of Article III', *Harvard Law Review*, 113 (2000), 924–1038, 1003.
[66] To some extent I believe that adjudication has been undermined by being inextricably linked in the minds of commentators and legal professionals with adversarialism. Authoritative judicial determination does not necessarily go hand in hand with unrestrained adversarialism – one only has to look at small-claims procedures or civilian jurisdictions to understand that.

it simply that sections of the judiciary feel themselves to be under increasing pressure? From the perspective of strained resources, growing caseloads, reducing levels of administrative support, increasing numbers of litigants in person who cannot afford legal representation and cannot obtain legal aid, the anti-litigation/anti-adjudication/pro-ADR story may begin to look attractive.

Conclusion

In the context of the increasing cost of criminal justice within a single justice budget, the government has been looking for ways of reducing expenditure on civil legal aid and the civil courts. A central plank of government policy on civil justice over the past decade has been to reduce the number of cases coming to the civil courts and to divert civil and commercial disputes into private dispute resolution. Although this policy has been given an 'access to justice' label it is, in fact, a policy directed at diverting disputes away from justice. Anti-law and anti-litigation rhetoric has assisted in downgrading the social value of the civil justice system as a means of developing and publicising the common law, while the emerging ADR profession has undermined adjudication with a postmodern argument that tells us that morally equivalent clashing interests are too complex for courts to decide, that there are no 'facts' that can be found in court and therefore no substance to which the coercive power of the state can be legitimately applied.

Leaving aside the philosophical question of whether there are any facts, is it helpful to conceive of civil disputes always in terms of 'problems', in a legal culture dominated by rights discourse? Most disputes or legal problems arise from the existence of a right or an obligation. For example, take my mother-in-law's stair lift which she bought a few months ago at considerable expense and which keeps sticking. The installers have twiddled with it, but it is still sticking. They refuse to come back again. She keeps getting stuck. Is this a problem involving a clash of morally equivalent interests – the installer's interest in not having to come out to fix it and my mother-in-law's interest in not getting stuck halfway up her stairs one night on the way to bed since she lives alone and is immobile? Or is this about the seller's obligation under the contract to ensure that the stair lift is in working order and my mother-in-law's right as a consumer to have a working stair lift? There have been telephone calls; there have been threats – to no avail. The next step will be a letter before action – a credible threat of invoking the power of the courts to direct the company to comply with its obligations. Do we think that they will mediate without that threat? Or is it the substantive law and the threat of coercive power that constitute the hand behind the back of the defendant prodding or pushing them towards fixing the stair lift or towards some settlement? In the context of this dispute, it is difficult to jettison rights or justice language. Justice is conceived of as the remedy that the substantive law offers. The peace language of mediation has nothing to do with substantive justice, but is about closure and possibly psychic healing. It is not about retribution or equity. It is about letting go of a grievance or wrong, in order to live in peace. This may be a valuable and indeed a necessary approach for nations in conflict, it may even be inevitable for aspects of disputes following relationship breakdown. But it has little resonance for my mother-in-law and her sticking stair lift.

I remember listening to the now Attorney General when she was a Minister in the LCD enthusiastically promoting ADR. She gave a speech in 2000 saying that in future the question that courts should be asking was not whether a case is suitable for diversion to ADR but why a case is thought suitable for adjudication. That is an interesting statement and a reflection of government thinking. Perhaps everything could be mediated and the courts could become pubs and restaurants, but should they, and realistically, if there were no courts why would any defendant agree to mediation?

Where, then, should ADR policy now be going? Policy in England continues to focus on how to encourage more people to mediate, how to divert more cases away from the courts. There is continued judicial pressure to mediate and a renewal of arguments for mandatory mediation.[67] Certainly, we should be facilitating mediation and educating people about the range of dispute resolution options. In a complex developed society it is entirely reasonable that we should have invented more than one way of resolving disputes. But once cases have been issued in court we should not be indiscriminately attempting to drive them away or compelling them, unwillingly, to enter into an additional process. I believe that policy on mediation requires more in the way of principled justification. Who

---

[67] Indeed at a conference in London in December 2008 entitled 'Civil Procedure Rules ten years on', one of the papers argued for the introduction of mandatory mediation along the lines of the Canadian system. See S. Prince, 'ADR after the CPR', Chapter 17 in D. Dwyer (ed.), *The Civil Procedure Rules Ten Years On* (Oxford University Press, 2009).

needs mediation and for what? Is it to reduce expenditure on the courts? Is it to provide more access to justice? Is it simply access to a quicker settlement? Or is it about encouraging harmony and moral growth?

There are also questions to be asked about the quality of the mediation process itself, which to date have tended to be left out of the litigation v mediation debate. The role of mediators is currently unregulated and they are unaccountable. The nature and extent of their responsibilities is not clearly articulated and ethical codes vary. These issues matter since mediators have considerable opportunity for the exercise of covert power during the course of mediations and in influencing settlement agreements.

As has been noted by a number of commentators, debate about mediation has a polarised feel about it. You are either for mediation or you are against it. Bryant Garth points to the impossibility of reconciling or harmonising these literatures and standpoints.[68]

> One side sounds positively nostalgic, invoking a romantic ideal of litigation culminating in a public trial with an authoritative pronouncement of public law. This ideal was useful when settlements were viewed as avoided trials. It is not so useful when trials are viewed as failed settlements.[69]

Mediation is constantly contrasted with adjudication, even though the most common form of civil case conclusion in

---

[68] B. Garth, 'From civil litigation to private justice: legal practice at war with the profession and its value', *Brooklyn Law Review*, 59 (1993), 931–60.

[69] Ibid, p. 957.

the UK and in many other jurisdictions is settlement.[70] In reviewing scholarly writing on ADR by proponents of mediation and proponents of adjudication I have come to the view that the opposing positions are, in the end, irreconcilable. That the proper question to be asking is not whether one wants peace or justice – because there can never be an answer for all cases. The challenge is in understanding that, in civil justice at least, there is an interdependency between the courts as publicisers of rules backed by coercive power, and the practice of ADR and settlement more generally. Without the background threat of coercion, disputing parties cannot be brought to the negotiating table. Mediation without the credible threat of judicial determination is the sound of one hand clapping. A well-functioning civil justice system should offer a choice of dispute resolution methods. We need modern, efficient civil courts with appropriate procedures that offer affordable processes for those who would choose judicial determination. This is not impossible. But it requires recognition of the social and economic value of civil justice, an acknowledgement that some cases need to be adjudicated, and a vision for reform that addresses perceived shortcomings rather than simply driving cases away.

[70] '... the "trial" was never the norm, never the modal way of resolving issues and solving problems in the legal system', L.M. Friedman, 'The day before trials vanished', *Journal of Empirical Legal Studies* 1:3 (2004), 689–703, 689.

4

Judges and civil justice

Few questions are as central to the study of the legal
process as that of how legal decisions are made. It is of
transcendent practical significance, because a favourable
decision is the presumed goal of every litigant. The
question also is an essential jurisprudential one, because
any theory of the nature of law necessarily embodies a
judgment about how law is made.[1]

Introduction

In this chapter I propose to continue the focus on
the social and economic significance of civil justice, but to
look more closely at adjudication or judicial determination
within that system. This has presented something of a challenge because of the scarcity of UK research on judicial behaviour. While there is scholarly writing on civil procedure and
research on legal services and advocacy, there is little written
on the role of the judge in civil justice, except as an adjunct to
the post-Woolf philosophy of adjudication – which required
the judiciary to change their culture, be less passive, roll up
their sleeves and get stuck into becoming case managers.

---

[1] J.M. Conley and W.M. O'Barr, 'Fundamentals of jurisprudence: an
ethnography of judicial decision making in informal courts', *North
Carolina Law Review*, 66 (1988), 467–508, 467.

My interest in the judicial role and judicial decision making arises from a number of sources. First, from having observed judges in courts and tribunal hearings during various research projects – often from the perspective of litigants, but also sitting with judges on the other side of the bench or table. This has given me a vivid sense of the expectations, fears and competence of litigants in court. It has also given me an insight into the day-to-day work of judges and, in particular, those below the waterline of the High Court.

The second source of my interest in how judges *do* justice comes from a long involvement with the Judicial Studies Board, where I have worked on the design and delivery of judicial training. As a result of watching judges and thinking about training and the changing nature of the judicial role, I have developed a keen interest in the challenges that the judiciary face in civil cases, how they do what they do and the pressures under which they increasingly and often, in my view heroically, work. This 'heroism' arises from the matters alluded to in earlier chapters involving pressure of work, little support, strained resources, little security, increasing numbers of unrepresented parties[2] and a disturbing trend in habitual litigants.

Most recently, and unsurprisingly, as a result of joining the Judicial Appointments Commission[3] (JAC) and working closely on the development of policies and practices

[2] R. Moorhead and M. Sefton, *Litigants in Person: Unrepresented Litigants in First Instance Proceedings* (Department for Constitutional Affairs, Research Series, 2005).
[3] This chapter is written in my personal capacity and does not represent JAC policy.

for the appointment of the judiciary in courts and tribunals, I have become even more interested in (if not positively *transfixed* by) the question of what makes a good judge. Not being a judge myself, and having the perspective that comes from researching the experiences of litigants and their lawyers, I have spent some time pondering what one wants from judges in different positions in the court structure, dealing with different types of cases and in light of judicial deployment policies that require judges to turn their hand to pretty much anything, and very quickly. I have also wondered about how best to devise recruitment and selection processes that will maximise the chances of appointing the best possible people from the widest range of backgrounds. In particular, I have thought hard about why diversity within the judiciary matters and whether the arguments about diversity should rest on dubious assertions of difference in approaches to decision making, or whether diversity issues are really about the legitimacy of the judiciary in a State governed by the rule of law. But I am not going to focus on diversity or the judicial appointments process in this chapter, except tangentially to ask how – having thought about the reality of the modern judicial role – it is possible to devise selection processes that are sufficiently nuanced to capture the full range of abilities that the judiciary require. I do, however, say a little more about diversity later in the chapter, drawing on the results of empirical studies of judicial decision making.

A final influence on the choice of topic, which also arises from working on judicial appointments, was a small but revealing piece of research that I have recently carried out for the Judicial Executive Board on what, to recently appointed judges and senior practitioners, is attractive and what is unattractive about moving on to the bench.[4] This is also discussed later in the chapter.

Another information 'black hole'

For each of these roles and activities (training, appointing and researching) the natural first step for an academic is always to read the literature. I wanted to read about the function of the judge in society – about judging as a social practice. I wanted to know about theories of judicial behaviour and decision making. I wanted to talk about how the job of the judge has changed in recent years (particularly post-Woolf) and about the ethical framework in which judicial decisions are taken. I was also interested about research on the impact of gender and ethnic background on judicial decision making. But I was struck by how little is known about the practice of judging, and even more striking, how little curiosity has been shown by UK academics about what seem to me to be pretty important issues.

A search of the UK literature on judicial decision making reveals a significant scholarly body of work closely analysing the decisions of the appellate courts, the ruminations and reprinted lectures of distinguished retired judges[5] and,

[4] H. Genn, *The Attractiveness of Senior Judicial Appointment to Highly Qualified Practitioners*, December 2008, Judicial Office for England, www.judiciary.gov.uk/docs/report-sen-jud-appt.pdf
[5] For example, Lord Woolf, *The Pursuit of Justice* (Oxford University Press, 2008); Lord Bingham, *The Business of Judging* (Oxford University Press, 2000); Lord Denning, *The Discipline of Law* (Oxford University Press, 1979); Lord Radcliffe, *Not in Feather Beds* (Hamilton, 1968); Lord Reid,

frankly, precious little else. There is a body of jurisprudential analysis of the written decisions of the senior judiciary, dealing with concepts such as neutrality and discretion and, interestingly, there is a significant body of research on the Law Lords.[6] To doctrinal scholars and constitutionalists, there can be little more fascinating than the opportunity not only to read and unpick the decisions of the highest appeal court but also to talk to the judges about how they reasoned their way through some of their more high-profile and difficult decisions. But the paradox is that while the written decisions of the senior judiciary have been highly scrutinised, the messy and more voluminous reality of judicial life in the trenches of the lower courts has been left almost entirely unexplored and therefore unanalysed and unexplained. There have been very few empirical studies in the UK of the work of the judiciary in

The Law and the Reasonable Man (Proceedings of the British Academy, 1968).

[6] As Penny Darbyshire notes in a forthcoming book (draft kindly made available), in contrast to the rest of the judiciary the House of Lords has been almost studied to death. She offers the following selection: Sir Louis Blom-Cooper and Gavin Drewry, *Final Appeal: A Study of the House of Lords in its Judicial Capacity* (Clarendon Press, 1972); Robert Stevens, *Law and Politics, The House of Lords as a Judicial Body 1800–1976* (University of North Carolina Press, 1978, UK edition 1979); Alan Paterson, *The Law Lords* (Clarendon Press, 1982); David Robertson, *Judicial Discretion in the House of Lords* (Clarendon Press, 1998); Paul Carmichael and Brice Dickson (eds), *The House of Lords: Its Parliamentary and Judicial Roles* (Hart Publishing 1999); Andrew Le Sueur (ed.) *Building the UK's New Supreme Court* (Oxford University Press, 2004) and *Constitutional Innovation: the creation of a Supreme Court for the United Kingdom; domestic, comparative and international reflections*, a special issue of *Legal Studies* (Oxford University Press, 2004) 24, issues 1 and 2, March 2004.

the county courts[7] or, with one or two exceptions, the High Court.[8] There is little that conveys the reality of county court judicial work and decision making, of the conditions in which the judiciary operate, how they go about their task, how they manage uncertainty, how they manage variable advocates, or no advocates, and how they seek to do justice. There is virtually nothing to be read on styles of judging, court behaviour, influences on decision making, managing the routine, managing the complex, the realities of life in court in the post-Woolf era, what approaches are effective for fact gathering, how credibility is assessed, what styles of communication work best with unrepresented parties.[9] There are snippets of information from small-scale observational studies in the county courts and tribunals,[10] but no major empirical studies of the work of

[7] Some notable exceptions appear in a recent special issue of *Social & Legal Studies* (2007), 16:3, on the subject of judgecraft. Some of this work is discussed later in the chapter.

[8] A recent exception is Varda Bondy and Maurice Sunkin, 'Accessing judicial review', *Public Law*, Winter (2008), 647–67. Analysing leave decisions in judicial review applications, the authors found a 'wide variation' in the grant rates among twenty-five judges, ranging from 46% to 11%. The authors suggest that there 'were no obvious factors to do with the nature or type of cases involved that would readily explain this wide variation', p. 665.

[9] R. Moorhead, M. Sefton and L. Scanlan, *Just Satisfaction? What Drives Public and Participant Satisfaction with Courts and Tribunals* (Ministry of Justice Research Series 5/08, 2008), p. 423.

[10] H. Genn et al. *Tribunals for Diverse Users* (Department for Constitutional Affairs, Research Series 1/06, 2006), involving observation and analysis of the behaviour and decisions of tribunal judiciary and interviews with tribunal judges; H. Genn and Y. Genn, *Representation in Tribunals* (Lord Chancellor's Department, 1989), involving analysis of decisions and comparison of decision making among tribunal judges;

the judiciary that enlighten us about their role. For example, there is very little discussion of fact-finding, even though this is a critical step in reaching decisions below the Court of Appeal. Deep within our legal culture, with its emphasis on orality, is the presumption that the seeing and hearing of witnesses is not merely useful but indeed crucial to accurate and fair judicial decisions. But how do civil judges sitting alone make vital assessments of credibility when there is a conflict of evidence? How do they assess whether a witness is lying or telling the truth and what techniques are there for improving credibility assessments? While research on lying shows incontrovertibly that most people are rather poor at detecting lies,[11] that the judiciary do no better than chance in experiments on detecting lies, and that demeanour is an unreliable guide to truth-telling, there is judicial authority for the proposition that demeanour is a legitimate factor to be taken into account in making an assessment of credibility.[12] Despite the importance

R. Moorhead and M. Sefton, *Litigants in Person*, involving observation of county court judiciary.

[11] See for example P. Ekman, *Telling Lies* (WW Norton & Co, 2001); D. McNeill, *The Face* (Hamish Hamilton, 1998), in particular Chapter 5, 'The lie and the veil'.

[12] Buxton, J. ' [The Adjudicator] had to look at the matter as a whole and in the light of the evidence that she gave and, not least and entirely properly, her demeanour when she was questioned by the adjudicator himself.' *Queen v Secretary of State for Home Department ex parte Arvinder Singh Virk* [1997] EWHC Admin 632 para. 13; 'I find her discrepancies or inconsistencies, or whatever term one may wish to use, as peripheral and comparatively speaking unimportant. My conclusion is that the essential part of her evidence is true. I have not the slightest doubt about it. She was quite unshaken either in content or demeanour on that essential and central evidence.' *R v Latimer* [2004] NICA 3.

and acknowledged difficulty of this aspect of the judicial role, little time is spent in judicial training discussing how assessments of credibility are and should be made and there is no research or scholarly literature addressing the issue. A notable exception here is Lord Bingham, who devoted the first chapter of his collected essays, *The Business of Judging*,[13] to the problem of finding facts and evaluating credibility. He remarks that 'to the judge, resolution of factual issues is (I think) frequently more difficult and more exacting than the deciding of pure points of law … He is dependent, for better or worse, on his own unaided judgment'.[14] Precisely because the subject is hard, and because on appeal such assessments are difficult to reconsider or dislodge, it is important to discuss how credibility is evaluated and which factors are legitimate and appropriate in reaching those assessments.

There is also no work that explores the relationship between judicial behaviour and public perceptions of fairness or confidence in the courts. What types of judicial behaviour contribute to perceptions of fairness or unfairness, satisfaction or acceptability or unacceptability of legal proceedings? The regular 'customer' surveys undertaken by the court service tell us a lot about the siting of coffee machines and the welcome given by clerks, but nothing of the central core of the court experience – what the judge did and said and what he or she decided in relation to this particular dispute. It is yet another black hole in our understanding of the operation of the justice system.

[13] Lord Bingham, *The Business of Judging*, Chapter 1, 'The judge as juror: the judicial determination of factual issues', pp. 3–24.
[14] Ibid, p. 3.

Not only has rigorous investigation not been under-taken, it seems that rarely is anyone even raising empirical questions about how judges work. This situation is frankly extraordinary and it is not true in other jurisdictions, nota-bly the USA, Canada, Australia and some parts of Europe.[15] Adjudication is seen as a fundamental social process that is of critical constitutional and democratic importance.[16]

> Although judges are servants of the public, they are not public servants. The tenure which they enjoy, the procedures which are required in the case of a proposal for their removal, and their institutional separateness from the executive arm of government, are all aimed at securing that position. The essential obligation of a public servant is, consistently with the law, to give effect to the policy of the government of the day. The duty of a judge is different. The duty of a judge is to administer justice according to law, without fear or favour, and without regard to the wishes or policy of the executive government.[17]

[15] For example, S. Roach Anleu and K. Mack, 'Magistrates' everyday work and emotional labour', *Journal of Law and Society*, 32: 4 (2005), 590–614; Gregory C. Sisk, Michael Heise and Andrew P. Morriss, 'Charting the influences on the judicial mind: an empirical study of judicial reasoning', *New York University Law Review*, 73 (1998), 1377; L. Epstein (ed.), *Courts and Judges* (Ashgate, 2005); L. Epstein and J. Knight, *The Choices Judges Make* (C.Q. Press, 1998).

[16] Resnik, 'Courts: in and out of sight, site and cite', *Villanova Law Review*, 53 (2008), 771–810.

[17] The Honourable Murray Gleeson AC, Chief Justice of Australia, *The Role of the Judge and Becoming a Judge*, National Judicial Orientation Programme, Sydney, 16 August 1998, www.hcourt.gov.au/speeches/cj/cj_njop.htm

US journals dealing with law, politics, psychology, sociology, law and economics regularly publish studies of judicial decision making – often at the appellate level, but also in District Courts.[18] American scholars, recognising the judiciary as the third arm of the State, have regarded judicial decision making as a legitimate and, indeed, essential subject for scholarly inquiry. Although some tentative steps have been taken relatively recently in England to explore the work of the judiciary in the lower courts[19] seeking to develop theories of 'judgecraft',[20] those undertaken in courts are small-scale, qualitative 'toes in the water' and we are a long way from a mature understanding of judicial behaviour in the trenches.

What I want to do in this chapter, apart from raising questions, is to suggest that the failure of the academy to scrutinise, describe and explain the work of judges is an astonishing void in our understanding of the essential functioning of the civil justice system. More importantly, it represents a void in understanding of the judiciary as a critical social institution,

---

[18] See the collection in L. Epstein (ed.), *Courts and Judges*.

[19] For example work on small claims by J. Baldwin, *Small Claims in County Courts in England and Wales: The Bargain Basement of Civil Justice?* (Clarendon Press, 1997); J. Baldwin, *Monitoring the Rise of the Small Claims Limit: Litigants' Experiences of Different Forms of Adjudication* (Lord Chancellor's Department, 1997); J. Baldwin, *Lay and Judicial Perspectives on the Expansion of the Small Claims Regime* (Lord Chancellor's Department Research Series 8/02, 2002); work on housing possession proceedings by D. Cowan and E. Hitchings, 'Pretty boring stuff: District Judges and housing possession proceedings', *Social & Legal Studies*, 16: 3 (2007), 363–82; R. Moorhead and M. Sefton, *Litigants in Person*.

[20] R. Moorhead and D. Cowan, 'Judgecraft: an introduction', *Social & Legal Studies*, 16: 3 (2007), 315–20; H.M. Kritzer, 'Toward a theorization of judgecraft', *Social & Legal Studies*, 16: 3 (2007), 321–40.

the legitimacy of which is fundamentally important in a State subject to the rule of law.

As I discussed in Chapters 1 and 2, set-piece trials may be only the tip (and a vanishing tip at that) of a very large dispute iceberg, but even so, many thousands of cases are processed and pass through the hands of the judiciary for management and interlocutory decisions even if they do not reach the stage of final adjudication. The hundreds of thousands of decisions made daily in the civil courts are part of 'the determination process'.[21] The sense that the *everyday* work of the judiciary is less worthy of study or less interesting than the decisions of the appeal courts is a reflection of the legal academy's preoccupation with the law, with its substance and its philosophical and moral foundations, rather than any particular interest in the *doing* of justice. It is arguable that rigorous empirical study of the thousands of everyday judicial determinations made in the lower courts would make it possible to identify patterns that cannot easily be detected in unsystematic reading of decisions[22] and would provide a more reliable indicator of judicial attitudes and behaviour than analysing the reasoning of the judiciary in the superior courts.[23]

How judges reason matters because it is the expression and application of legal principles. But what judges *do* – i.e. what

---

[21] Ibid, p. 316.

[22] G.C. Sisk, 'The quantitative moment and the qualitative opportunity: legal studies of judicial decision making' (book review), *Cornell Law Review*, 93: 2 (2008), 873.

[23] See F.B. Cross, *Decision Making in the U.S. Courts of Appeals* (Stanford University Press, 2007).

judges decide – in the everyday cases that come before the courts matters in terms of the objectives of civil justice (fair and just dispute resolution according to law, social order, stability and certainty of business transactions) as well as public expectations of courts, public confidence in courts and public perceptions of fair procedure.

Kate Malleson has argued that the lack of research on judicial behaviour is less a failure of interest on the part of legal scholars and more a reflection of the judiciary's resistance to co-operating with research.[24] If that was ever really true, I believe that it has not been true for quite a while. While the judiciary are, like other professional groups, somewhat cautious about providing access to researchers, the very small number of studies recently undertaken involving judicial co-operation demonstrates the possibility of undertaking such work. In any case, there is nothing to prevent observational research in open court. Anyone at any time could undertake observation of judicial behaviour. It is just rarely done.

I think that the focus on written decisions occurs for several reasons. First, they are freely available so it takes no effort to collect the raw material for research. Second, most doctrinal legal scholars have neither the interest nor the skills to undertake research on judicial behaviour rather than judicial reasoning. Marc Galanter has argued that legal academics are enchanted by 'text' rather than 'context' and that they mirror the intellectual styles of both judges and lawyers. 'Like judges they privilege legal doctrine and justification. Like

---

[24] K. Malleson, *The New Judiciary: The Effects of Expansion and Activism* (Ashgate Press, 1999), pp. 196–7.

lawyers they are more interested in the critical deconstruction of opposing arguments than in the collaborative process of describing, explaining and exploring the legal world.'[25] Third, political scientists and other social scientists in the UK who do have the necessary repertoire of research skills have shown no interest in the judiciary, or indeed the legal system as a whole, as a subject for research. This seems to me to be a remarkable and dispiriting failure on the part of social science to engage with one of the most obvious sites of power within the modern state. It may be a reflection of certain deep socio-political assumptions that the law somehow does not count. Or it may be that lawyers have successfully repelled incursions by communicating that law is just too hard, too impenetrable – unknowable except by its self-referential self and its own.

But why should this research be done? The judiciary may not feel that there is any particular urgency for the wider world to have a better understanding of how they go about their work and how they reach their decisions. Yet parts of the judiciary, for example in the world of tribunals, have shown themselves highly receptive to, even encouraging of, research that would help them enhance judicial skills and understand better the process of panel decision making. I also believe that there are many self-reflective judges, keen to improve their skills, who would be interested in a deeper empirical understanding of the judicial function.

---

[25] M. Galanter, 'In the winter of our discontent: law, anti-law and social science', *Annual Review of Law and Social Science*, 2 (2006), 1–16, 11.

Jerome Frank, the distinguished American judge and legal scholar, wrote almost sixty years ago:

> I am unable to conceive that … in a democracy it can ever be unwise to acquaint the public with the truth about the workings of any branch of government … The best way to bring about the elimination of those shortcomings of our judicial system which are capable of being eliminated is to have all our citizens informed as to how that system now functions.[26]

More recently the controversial judge Richard Posner has also argued robustly that a better understanding of judicial behaviour is essential.

> Judges like other 'refined' people in our society are reticent about talking about sex, but judges are also reticent about talking about judging … This reticence makes the scholarly study of judicial behaviour at once challenging and indispensable.[27]

It seems to me that there are several justifications for developing a field of empirical judicial studies in England. The first is academic. The judiciary is a critical social institution supporting economic activity, protecting large and small rights, deciding large and small issues that bear directly on policy. How can we operate in ignorance of how it goes about its work? Moreover, institutions do not stand still; they are subject to change and flux. The English judiciary has a high reputation around the world, but what is it that supports that

[26] J. Frank, *Courts on Trial, Myth and Beauty in American Justice* (Princeton University Press, 1949), pp. 2–3.
[27] R.A. Posner, *How Judges Think* (Harvard University Press, 2008), p. 6.

reputation and how do we prevent its corrosion. As Aharon Barak (presumably alluding to Alexander Hamilton's statement in the US Federalist Papers No. 78) has observed: 'An essential condition for realizing the judicial role is public confidence in the judge ... [T]he judge has neither sword nor purse. All he has is the public's confidence in him.'[28]

Another justification for knowing more about how the judiciary goes about its work is a question of legitimacy.[29] We need some understanding of the relationship between judicial behaviour, court users' perceptions of the fairness of proceedings and public confidence in and respect for the judiciary. Which aspects of judicial behaviour tend to increase the reputation of the judiciary and which aspects tend to undermine its reputation and standing? While the government, judiciary and others are happy to make assumptions about public confidence in the courts, we have even less information about public perceptions or experiences of the judiciary than we do about the activities of the judiciary. In the UK we have little idea about how the public views the courts, other than through the lens of criminal justice,[30] and interestingly, although the situation is a little better in the USA,[31] many other jurisdictions

[28] A. Barak *The Judge in a Democracy* (Princeton University Press, 2006), p. 109.
[29] S.M. Olson and D.A. Huth, 'Explaining public attitudes toward local courts', *Justice System Journal*, 20 (1998), 41.
[30] H. Genn, *Paths to Justice* (Hart Publishing, 1999). 'When people think about courts it is always the criminal courts'; Moorhead, Sefton and Scanlan (*Just Satisfaction?*) confirm this absence of information about civil justice.
[31] D.B. Rottman, *Public Trust and Confidence in the State Courts: A Primer* (National Center for State Courts, Working Paper, March 1999); *How the Public Views the State Courts: A 1999 National Survey* (National Center for State Courts, May 1999).

experience the same lack of information. A recent review of attitudes towards the justice system in the UK and Europe confirms the absence of information relating to perceptions of civil justice and notes that existing survey data generally focus on the criminal justice system or the justice system in general without distinguishing civil justice issues.

> For the civil element of the justice system, there is considerably less data available. Where such information exists, it often consists of localised ad-hoc surveys. When citizens have been asked about the justice system in general, they have usually thought first about judges in criminal cases. This is an internationally significant tendency.[32]

The authors of a study of public perceptions of the Canadian judiciary undertaken for the Canadian civil justice review in 2005 remarked: 'We found surprisingly little research specifically about public perceptions of the judiciary or related issues. An overall conclusion is that we actually have very little reliable and valid evidence … about public views of the Canadian judiciary or even about the justice system in general, in any detail.'[33]

A third justification for research on judicial behaviour is instrumental. A better understanding of the realities of judging, particularly in the trenches, would improve our ability to appoint the right people to the right jobs. There is not

[32] S. Van de Walle and J.W. Raine, *Explaining Attitudes Towards the Justice System in the UK and Europe* (Ministry of Justice Research Series, 9/08, 2008), p. 47.
[33] M. Stratton, 'Public perceptions of the role of the Canadian judiciary', *The Canadian Forum on Civil Justice* (December 2005), p. 6. http://cfcj-fcjc.org/docs/2005/cjsp-perceptions-en.pdf

one effective style of judging. There is not one effective type of judge. There is a vast range of approaches and techniques, suitable in different circumstances. Effective communication and enabling depends on judges being able to 'fit' their approach to the situation and parties before them. Even in the High Court a judge will one day face opposing Silks of the highest quality and another day have a Silk of the highest quality and an unrepresented party. The contexts require different methods if both sides are to be dealt with fairly. If we had a deeper understanding, or indeed any understanding, of the range of qualities and abilities needed for diverse parts of the judicial system, including what have been referred to as the 'capillaries' of the legal system[34] – we would be better able to refine selection criteria and selection methods. Greater insight into the work and decision-making processes of the judiciary at the coalface would enrich judicial training and offer the possibility of more nuanced programmes. The recruitment of judges from a much wider range of backgrounds than has historically been the case offers an opportunity to explore whether backgrounds other than in advocacy bring different experiences and skills sets to the bench and to analyse whether these influence the approach to case handling and decision making. Fascinating and, I would argue, critical as these questions are, their investigation is not on the horizon.

Without a description and understanding of the *everyday* work and decisions of the judiciary at all levels (or positive analysis of what they do) it is difficult to articulate a normative

[34] M.A. Glendon, *A Nation Under Lawyers* (Harvard University Press, 1996). She refers to judges in the lower courts as 'judges in the capillaries of the legal system', pp. 168–9.

and ethical framework for the realities of modern judging within the civil justice system. It is also difficult to understand what impact increased pressures within civil justice might have on the practice of judging, on judges themselves and on their job satisfaction. A better understanding of the influences and pressures on decision making in the civil courts matters critically in the context of increasing strain on civil justice, decreasing resources and degrading courts. Would such research tend to reduce public confidence in the judiciary or, more likely, might it tend to raise questions about the support and the resources that the judiciary receives?

The significance of the judiciary in civil justice

It is generally accepted – and certainly by the World Bank – that a well-functioning civil justice system is important for social order and healthy economies. Courts promulgate and reinforce important social values, thus underpinning social order and stability. They are also capable of reflecting and promoting social change, by supporting and underlining changing norms and social processes. As Epstein argues, judicial decisions often represent a critical stage in the process of changing social norms and developing public policy. Issues of public policy may appear in the courts for judicial determination on several occasions before the issue is finally either settled or 'superseded by new problems of public policy'.[35]

---

[35] L. Epstein, Introduction, *Courts and Judges* (Ashgate, 2005) p. xx.

There is a worldwide political consensus that 'transparent adjudicatory processes are a prerequisite to successful market-based democracies'[36] and that institutions focused on development have seen law as pivotal to the functioning of markets.[37] It is recognised that thriving market economies depend on a strong State that will secure private property rights. But a State that is strong enough to secure property rights also has the strength to appropriate them – see the example of Russia. An independent judiciary that can hold the government to account is therefore economically important. Economists have quantified the value of a strong, independent and incorrupt judiciary, calculating the positive influence on gross domestic product (GDP) and economic growth.[38] But the same economists argue that *de jure* independence – the formal position of the judiciary – is not what is important. What matters is *de facto* independence – indicators that demonstrate independence and quality in practice. In analysing the factors that support the strength and quality of independent judiciaries, *Transparency International*[39] draws attention to the general culture of societies and whether there is endemic corruption – but also specific factors that are capable of supporting or threatening the independence and probity of the

[36] J. Resnik, 'Migrating, morphing, *and* vanishing: the empirical and normative puzzles of declining trial rates in courts', *Journal of Empirical Legal Studies*, 1: 3 (2004), 783–841, 785.

[37] Ibid, p. 811.

[38] S. Voight, 'Economic growth, certainty in the law and judicial independence', in Transparency International, *Global Corruption Report 2007: Corruption in Judicial Systems*, (Cambridge University Press, 2007), p. 24.

[39] *Global Corruption Report 2007*, pp. xxiv–xxv.

judiciary. These include the resources allocated to the functioning of the courts, remuneration of the judiciary and political interference. Thus dwindling resources are identified as a factor that can pose a threat to the judiciary. Indeed, theories of institutional corrosion and decline[40] suggest that organisations do not stand still and that pressures introduced through resource constraints can lead to dissatisfaction and organisational entropy.

The English judiciary have, at least in modern times if not always, enjoyed a global reputation for intellectual quality and high standards of probity. This is not true of other jurisdictions and it is something that I believe we take for granted. The English civil courts, judges and English law, in particular commercial law, are an important invisible export. English law is the contractual law of choice for many overseas commercial enterprises and many foreign companies choose to bring their disputes to the Commercial Court in London. If one looks at the annual Global Corruption reports one sees that public perceptions of the judiciary in the UK compare well with most other jurisdictions (although not as well as Denmark, Sweden or Finland) – see Figure 4.1.

Recent surveys of public attitudes in the UK show that the public is willing to express high levels of trust that the judiciary will tell the truth, third only to family doctors and headteachers (82 per cent said that they would generally trust judges to tell the truth, compared with 83 per cent for headteachers and 94 per cent for family doctors – see

---

[40] J. Kleinig, 'Judicial corrosion: outlines of a theory', Conference on Confidence in the Judiciary, Canberra, February 2007.

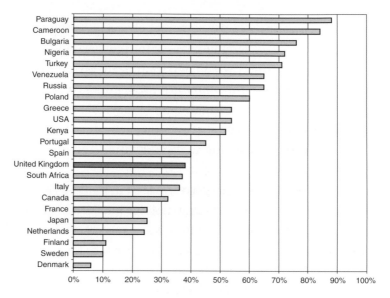

Figure 4.1 Percentage who describe their judiciary/legal system as corrupt

Source: Global Corruption Report 2007: Corruption in Judicial Systems

Figure 4.2)[41] a pattern that has held good over the three years of the survey and has been replicated in other studies of public trust. The reputation of English law and the courts is to a large extent based on a foundation of respect and trust in the English judiciary. How reputations are formed is a complex business, but it is true that while reputations can be made, they can also be lost. That is why appointing judges of the highest calibre and ensuring that candidates of the highest calibre put themselves forward for consideration is critical. This is about

[41] *Survey of Public Attitudes Towards Conduct in Public Life 2008* (Committee on Standards in Public Life, 2008).

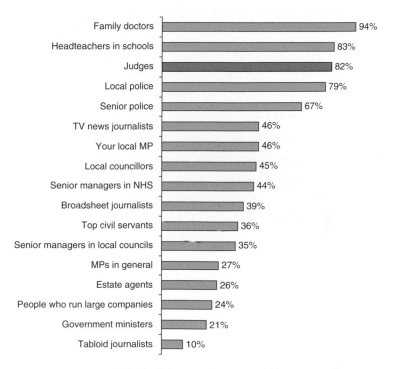

Figure 4.2 Which of these professions would you generally trust to tell the truth?

Source: CSPL 2008 Public Attitudes Survey

securing the quality of the judiciary for the future and ensuring that it performs to the highest standards. As Lord Woolf has pointed out: 'The standard of justice in a particular jurisdiction … continues to depend primarily upon the quality of its judges.'[42] If this was always the case, the need for quality is even more urgent in light of the increased power of the judiciary in the twentieth century.

[42] Lord Woolf, *The Pursuit of Justice*.

Twentieth-century growth in judicial power

There is general agreement among legal scholars and political scientists that, since the end of the Second World War, and with mounting speed during the past forty years, there has been a marked increase in the power of the judiciary in both the common law world and some civilian jurisdictions – trends referred to as increasing legalisation of the social world and a shift from democracy to 'juristocracy'.[43] The shift can be traced to a number of sources, some of which were discussed in Chapter 2 – an expansion of legal remedies, the establishment of the welfare state, growth of the legal profession and more legal challenges to business and public bodies.

Second, there has been a growth in judicial review and, in continental Europe, in the power to review laws for constitutionality. Equally importantly, academics have pointed to the modern trend in some countries, including England, for major political controversies to end up in the courts, decided by judges, rather than by elected legislators. While theories about the causes of this tendency are beyond the scope of this book, I stress the point because this power exercised by the judiciary through the civil courts exposes the judiciary to conflict with the executive and attracts significant media

[43] R. Hirschl, *Towards Juristocracy: The Origins and Consequences of the New Constitutionalism* (Harvard University Press, 2004); C. Guarneri and P. Pederzoli, *From Democracy to Juristocracy? The Power of Judges: A Comparative Study of Courts and Democracy*, (Oxford University Press, 2002); L. Friedman Goldstein, 'From democracy to juristocracy', *Law and Society Review*, 38 (2004), 611–29.

attention. Flash points in recent years have been security issues and immigration control. The increased visibility of the judiciary in social policy issues and in areas previously regarded as an arena for political rather than judicial decision making has made the question of who is appointed to the judiciary and how they are appointed, what they do, what they decide and how they reach their decisions a matter of public interest and of political debate.[44]

Third, it is arguable that the post-Woolf transformation of civil justice – with its emphasis on efficiency and case management, with the decline of public trials, with the increasing caseloads and pressure for rapid case processing – has increased judicial discretion and therefore the power of judges. This increased discretion is not so much in relation to the high-visibility cases that might be the subject of media comment, but in the hundreds of thousands of procedural and substantive determinations that are made away from the kind of public scrutiny that Bentham argued kept the judge, while trying, himself on trial.[45]

Finally, modern developments have also increased the *reach* of the judiciary into areas far removed from traditional legal fields. An example, cited less frequently than judicial review, is the field of medical decision making.

[44] J. Allan, 'Judicial appointments in New Zealand', Chapter 5 in K. Malleson and P.H. Russell (eds), *Appointing Judges in an Age of Judicial Power* (University of Toronto Press, 2006), pp. 108–9.

[45] See for example Michael Zander's recent criticisms of judicial inconsistency as a result of increased judicial discretion: 'More harm than good', *New Law Journal*, March (2009).

Advances in medicine and medical technology have raised
ethical challenges not previously contemplated. In the realms
of life and death, and leaving aside the issue of abortion, matters of extreme ethical seriousness are left to be decided by
the judiciary in situations where there are deep and strongly
held divisions in public opinion arising from differing fundamental religious, cultural and social values. A classic example was the Court of Appeal decision, in September 2000,
whether to allow the conjoined twins, Jodie and Mary, to
be separated when it would cause the certain death of one.[46]
The difficulty of the decision and the conflicting ethical positions were reflected in Lord Justice Ward's introduction to his
judgment:

> In the past decade an increasing number of cases have
> come before the courts where the decision whether or not
> to permit or to refuse medical treatment can be a matter
> of life and death for the patient. I have been involved in
> a number of them. They are always anxious decisions to
> make but they are invariably eventually made with the
> conviction that there is only one right answer and that the
> court has given it.
>
> In this case the right answer is not at all as easy to find.
> I freely confess to having found it exceptionally difficult
> to decide – difficult because of the scale of the tragedy
> for the parents and the twins, difficult for the seemingly
> irreconcilable conflicts of moral and ethical values and
> difficult because the search for settled legal principle has

[46] *Re A (Children)* [2000] EWCA Civ 254.

150

been especially arduous and conducted under real pressure of time.[47]

These are issues about which views legitimately differ and about which positions may be entrenched and polarised. They are issues of profound social significance with long-lasting impact, which have been delegated to the judiciary, presumably because they are too sensitive and difficult for politicians to deal with. As Hirschl has convincingly argued, the rise of the 'juristocracy' does not necessarily occur because hyperactive judges seize power from political power holders.[48] Political choices and interests are crucial factors in explaining the origins of judicial activism. He argues that, from the politician's point of view, delegating policy-making authority to the courts can be an effective way of shifting responsibility and deflecting the risks inherent in difficult areas. Hirschl refers to this as politicians' simple 'blame defection' strategy in which delegation of powers benefits politicians if it can reduce the blame attributed to the politician. 'The transfer to the courts of contested political "hot potatoes" ... offers a convenient retreat for politicians who have been unwilling or unable to settle contentious public disputes in the political sphere.'[49]

One of the consequences of shifting reputational risk from politicians to the judiciary is that high-profile decisions with significant moral, ethical and policy implications focus a bright spotlight on the judiciary. Almost inevitably, at some

---

[47] Ibid, per Lord Ward, at para. VI (I), 'Introduction to the case of the Siamese twins'.

[48] R. Hirschl, 'Juristocracy – Political, not Juridical', *The Good Society*, 13, No. 3 (2004).

[49] Ibid, p. 8.

point the questions are asked (and generally by the *Daily Mail*): 'Who is this judge? What is his background? How does he speak for society? Is it right for that decision to be made by an appointed official rather than an elected representative? How was he appointed and who did the appointing?'

Interest in the composition of the judiciary

In this context of increased curiosity about the background of the judiciary, the homogeneity of the senior levels of the judiciary becomes very evident. Contemporary political interest in judicial diversity can be seen as a collision of separate social currents which have combined to focus attention on the gender and ethnic composition of the judiciary. There has been a demand for a more tolerant and inclusive society and a demand for changes in traditional power structures so that the grip of white males is loosened to allow entry to power of women and minorities. But the increased attention on judicial diversity also reflects the growing power of the judiciary over the course of the twentieth century. If the judiciary is seen as the third arm of government, then concern about lack of diversity is less a question of whether women and minority ethnic groups might decide cases differently than white males, and more about participation in power. The argument for increasing the diversity of the judiciary should not, in my view, rest on specious assumptions about different group styles or approaches to decision making – do women see things differently from men? Do minorities have different values? Do they better understand the experiences of the population? To some extent I think that what is called the 'business case' for increasing the diversity of the judiciary is patronising, irrelevant and undermining. In any case, it is largely anti-empirical. As discussed later in the chapter, US studies of judicial decision making show that race, gender, personal values and preferences have only a weak and inconsistent influence on judicial decision making as compared with orientation to legal policy, the desire to impress various audiences for judicial decisions, group dynamics of panel judging and, not unimportantly, the desire not to have to work over the weekend. There will be as many differences *within* groups in styles of decision making as *between* groups (and the US literature supports that view). Moreover, the idea that even all white males demonstrate an undifferentiated approach to decision making is plainly absurd.

The diversity question is fundamentally about the judiciary as a central institution in a liberal representative democracy governed by the rule of law. It is simply no longer acceptable for an institution of such power and influence to appear to exclude well-qualified candidates who are neither male nor white (nor barristers). The shortage of women and minority ethnic judges, in particular in more senior positions, is and should be interpreted as exclusion from power. The diversity issue is about participation in powerful practices. It is about participation in the small and large decisions that shape the society in which we live. In my view it is unnecessary to make the 'business case' for increasing the diversity of the judiciary by seeking to establish that women decide differently from men or that people with a dark skin tone who were born and educated in the UK have a different perspective on the world from white men. They may do, but it is not relevant to the fundamental point. It is enough to say that there are well-qualified candidates from underrepresented groups who should be appointed to the bench. How this is achieved is a different question and beyond the scope of this chapter.

Which judges?

> Judges perform their work in majestic courthouses, decrepit buildings, small hearing rooms, and their offices or chambers. Some judges spend most of their time working in a single building, while others travel from place to place to handle cases in a variety of communities. Advocates appearing before judges include accomplished specialists, struggling beginners, and inarticulate self-represented litigants. Throughout all of the variations, we expect judges to act with intelligence, dignity, neutrality, respect, compassion, and efficiency. The challenges facing judges are immense, and judges are remarkably successful in responding to and meeting those challenges.[50]

A principal trap in talking about 'the judiciary' is that of scope and generalisation. When we refer to 'the judiciary', which judges are we talking about? In Chapter 1, I noted that one of the problems of theorising about civil justice was the variety and critical differences in the kinds of cases that come before the civil courts. The action for judicial review where the government or public body is being called to account raises different questions and has a different public significance from the case of the individual about to be

---

[50] H.M. Kritzer, 'Toward a theorization of craft', 321–40, 321–2.

evicted from their home – although the impact for the individual may be more catastrophic in the latter case. Similarly, when we discuss 'judges', are we thinking principally of the High Court and above, the circuit bench and below or the uniform branch as a whole? Or do we include tribunals and lay magistrates? Judges at all of these levels are performing similar, although distinct, tasks. But in practice, the burdens, pressures and skills vary depending on the area of the court system in which you are placed. The judges in civil justice that tend to grab the headlines are those in the High Court and above. The pace of their work is quite different from much of the work in the county courts – which is where the stuff of everyday legal problems is dealt with. These courts deal with a large volume of cases, although a diminishing number of set-piece trials. Work is characterised by rapid processing, often in the absence of counsel or with the disadvantage of counsel of highly variable quality. Judges depend on their experience and sometimes just their wits. There is little time for reflection and the caseload covers an enormous range. The District Judge in the County Court will have a diet of cases covering family, insolvency, personal injury, small claims, possession proceedings and cases will be listed for as few as five minutes. In some circumstances, the work of the judiciary appears more like high-speed social work than adjudication. But here, just as much as in the more rarefied atmosphere of the Royal Courts, the judiciary are seeking to 'do justice'. As Mary Ann Glendon has argued, the unique role of the highest courts requires a different set of qualities than that demanded of lower courts, which she describes as the 'heroism of sticking to one's last, of demonstrating impartiality, interpretive skill and responsibility toward authoritative sources in the regular administration of justice.[51] Justice in the trenches.

Unfortunately, there is no domestic evidence to provide a convincing description of the different skills and qualities needed respectively in the High Court and the trenches of the county courts. The most substantial literature on judicial behaviour emanates from North America and principally concerns judges in the higher courts. It is, nonetheless, instructive to review what has been learned elsewhere in order to provide a framework for thinking about judicial behaviour and decision making and reflecting on the work, pressures and threats to the judiciary in England and, in particular, in the lower courts.

Understanding judicial behaviour in the higher courts

As discussed earlier, a major project of US political science has been the attempt to understand and explain judicial decision making in relation to the ideological and other preferences of the judiciary. This work has been conducted in a climate where the selection and performance of the judiciary is overtly political and where the politics of the senior judiciary is a critical variable in the analysis of decision making. There is a wealth of studies by US social scientists seeking to unravel the various influences on judicial decisions and, in particular, the extent to which the characteristics of the person deciding

---

[51] M.A. Glendon, *A Nation Under Lawyers.*

determine *what* is decided.[52] This work has produced a number of models of judicial decision making[53] that can be helpful in untangling some of the influences on judicial behaviour.[54]

Despite the inevitable worry about extrapolating from the USA, where the political affiliation of the senior judiciary is a matter of public debate and where some judges are elected rather than appointed, in the absence of any home-grown research it is interesting quickly to survey the learning from across the Atlantic. Scholars have described either three models of judicial behaviour or possibly as many as nine – depending on whom you read. The three most common models have been labelled as 'legal', 'attitudinal' and 'strategic'.[55]

The *legal* model of judicial decision making suggests that in reaching their decisions judges are principally, or solely, motivated by a desire to interpret the law as well

[52] For a review of some of this literature, see G.C. Sisk, M. Heise and A.P. Morriss, 'Charting the influences on the judicial mind: an empirical study of judicial reasoning' *New York University Law Review*, 73 (1998), 1377–500.

[53] For a summary of the approaches see L. Baum, *Judges and Their Audiences* (Princeton University Press, 2006), Chapter 1. See also R. Posner, *How Judges Think*, pp. 19–56.

[54] Interestingly, and in support of the view that the legal academy has shunned the opportunity to research what judges do as opposed to how they reason, in reviewing and commenting on some of the theoretical insights that have been gained from empirical research on judging, Richard Posner has noted that despite its richness, the literature on judicial behaviour has been ignored by most academic lawyers and 'by virtually all judges'. R.A. Posner, 'What do judges and justices maximize? (The same thing everybody else does)', *Supreme Court Economic Review*, 3 (1993), 1–41, 7.

[55] L. Baum, *Judges and Their Audiences*, Chapter 1.

as possible. 'Judicial decisions are determined by "the law",
conceived of as a body of pre-existing rules found stated in
canonical legal materials, such as constitutional and statutory
texts and previous decisions of the same or a higher court, or
derivable from those materials by logical operations.'[56] Thus
the choice between alternative possible case outcomes and
doctrinal positions is primarily based on the judge's view of
the legal merits of the case according to his reading of the law.
This is the judiciary's 'official' theory of judicial behaviour.
It hypothesises that judicial decisions are determined by the
law – the idea of government of laws not men. The legal model
is about objectivity and impartiality and visualises the law as
an autonomous discipline in which rules are given and have
only to be applied. The vision of the judge operating according
to the legal model of judicial decision making is what Baum
has termed the judge as 'Vulcan'[57] – uninfluenced by emotion,
unperturbed by personal preferences and unaffected by consequentialist anxieties.

Although forests of paper have been sacrificed in
debates between different legal philosophical camps about the
extent to which the legal model does, could, should or would
ever fully explain judicial decisions, it remains the dominant
and official explanation for how judges come to their decisions

[56] R.A. Posner, *How Judges Think,*. p. 41.
[57] L. Baum, *Judges and Their Audiences*, p. 9. It is an allusion to the science
fiction series *Star Trek*, which features a humanoid species known as
Vulcans, who come from the planet Vulcan. The chief Vulcan character
is Mr Spock. Vulcans are noted for their attempt to live by reason and
logic with no interference from emotion. What is interesting is that they
are not intended to be *without* emotion, but rather engaged in a constant
internal struggle to *control* emotion.

in most cases. Richard Posner is scathing about the purist legalist explanation and its deficiencies in failing to provide normative guidance to judges as to how they should exercise judgement when dealing with policy decisions and providing an excuse for the judiciary to remain impervious to the wider context in which decisions must be made. 'The legalist judge is uninterested professionally in social science, philosophy or any other possible source of guidance for making policy judgments, because he is not engaged, or at least he thinks he is not engaged in making such judgments.' Taken to its logical conclusion, Posner argues that it is not even necessary for a purely legalist judge to have good judgement, to be wise, to be experienced or to be mature. If all that is required is for a judge to be a logician, then none of these qualities is necessary.[58]

The *attitudinal* model is the legal realist's challenge to the legal model. It claims that judges make decisions based in part on their personal policy preferences rather than solely according to the law. As a result, their choice between alternative outcomes is influenced by their view of the merits in relation to their broad policy preferences.

A variant of the attitudinal model is what Posner calls the *psychological approach*. This focuses on strategies for coping with uncertainty and how judges' preconceptions may shape response to uncertainty. The *behavioural* (or social attribute) approach looks at the extent to which social factors and personal values influence decisions. 'Nothing is more common than for different people of equal competence in reasoning to form different beliefs from the same information.'[59]

[58] R.A. Posner, *How Judges Think*, p. 42.
[59] R.A. Posner, *How Judges Think*, p. 97.

The evidence here is mixed, suggesting that some social and psychological factors can, in some circumstances and in relation to some sorts of cases, influence judicial decisions. In the world of the attitudinal/behavioural judge the outcome of a case for any particular litigant is a matter of who decided the case on the day. As Jeremy Waldron has pointed out, it is a matter of being 'lucky in your judge':

> On the realist and [Critical Legal Studies] accounts, legal outcomes are determined arbitrarily, relative to the right sort of reason. They are determined by factors – like the personal or political preferences of judges, or what the judge had for breakfast, or what happened to him in the lavatory when he was two years old, or whether the altruism neuron fired during an individualist process of reasoning – factors that really have nothing to do with the sort of reasons we want to operate.[60]

For example, a recent study in the United States found that young judges were less sympathetic to age-discrimination claimants than the oldest judges, although only at the extreme ends of the age spectrum.[61]

Despite the huge interest in the influence of attitudes on judicial decisions, studies of the impact of social attributes on judicial decision making are inconsistent and there is growing evidence that the 'orientation' of the judge into the judicial role is equally and possibly more important than social factors

[60] Jeremy Waldron, 'Lucky in your judge', *Theoretical Inquiries in Law*, 9: 1 (January 2008), 185–216, 206.
[61] K.L. Manning, B.A. Carroll and R. A. Carp, 'Does age matter? Judicial decision making in age discrimination cases', *Social Science Quarterly*, 85:1 (March 2004), 1–18.

(suggesting the importance of the training of the judiciary). Where judges are appointed from practice, it seems that legal education is critical to how they reason, their ethical orientation and their commitment to judicial values.[62]

It is worth mentioning here the efforts that have been made to assess the impact of race and gender on judicial decision making. The result has been unconvincing. For the most part, empirical research has failed to support the claim that minority judges have assumed an advocacy role on behalf of any racially based interests. Studies of trial judges in the context of criminal cases and criminal sentencing have uncovered very little variation in the behaviour of judges based upon race. For this reason, some researchers have concluded that legal or judicial socialisation or the judicial recruitment process 'screen[s] out those candidates with unconventional views'.[63] The alternative explanation is that race is *not* a driving force for judicial behaviour, but instead that in most cases 'the law – not the judge – dominates the outcome'.[64] In fact, the conclusion of behavioural studies is that judicial decision making is so complex, and the difficulty of creating realistic experiments so challenging, that it is difficult to conclude anything other than that the constraints of precedent, concern about internal criticism through appeal and interest in promotion are more consistently important in predicting judicial decisions (below the Supreme Court) than any particular social or demographic factors.

---

[62] See G.C. Sisk et al. 'Charting the influences on the judicial mind', for a review of US studies.

[63] Ibid, p. 1455.

[64] Ibid, p. 1456.

The *strategic* model of judicial behaviour also focuses on judges' policy preferences, but in terms of the best outcome for the court or the government as a whole. It is essentially a consequentialist model. Strategic judges consider the effects of their choices on collective outcomes, in their own court and in the broader judicial and policy arenas. They do not just do the right thing in the instant case; they want to advance long-term goals. Thus the strategic model suggests that judicial decisions are influenced by the anticipated reaction of other judges, legislators and even the public.

There is also what Posner calls a *sociological* model which focuses on small-group dynamics and is most relevant for judges who sit in panels. This account of influences on judicial behaviour suggests that the ultimate decision is likely to be influenced not only by the preferences and values of the members of the panel but also by the intensity with which members of the panel feel a preference for one outcome or another. You might prefer one result, but do you care enough to dissent, or are you happy to go along with what the others decide? This can also be compounded by what Posner terms 'dissent aversion'. Judges might not like to dissent because it involves more work, frays collegiality and magnifies the importance of the majority decision. 'Dissent aversion reflects the simultaneous difficulty and importance of collegiality. Appellate judging is a cooperative enterprise.'[65]

The *economic theory* of judicial behaviour treats the judge as a rational, self-interested utility maximiser. In Posner's words, judges are 'all too human workers responding as

[65] R.A. Posner, *How Judges Think*, p. 33.

JUDGES AND CIVIL JUSTICE

other workers do to the conditions of the labour market in which they work'.[66] He has argued that judges are not a collection of 'genius saints' miraculously immune to the tug of self-interest; instead, they are ordinary people subject to the same incentives and motivations as others.[67] It has been suggested that the attractions of office that influence decision making are popularity among the profession (a key audience for decisions), prestige, avoiding reversal and reputation. Judges may also behave in a way that is likely to increase leisure time or avoid hassle. Posner suggests that when judges sit together, their behaviour is influenced by a range of non-legal factors and that concurrence may be a manifestation of leisure-seeking rather than power-maximising behaviour. He suggests that an objective for future research on judicial behaviour would be to attempt to disentangle self-interest from other motivations and judicial doctrines and practices.[68]

While judges also obtain satisfaction from the exercise of power in making decisions, they are also motivated by the 'intrinsic pleasure of writing … and displaying analytical prowess or other intellectual gifts, for those who have them and want to use them'. This view is supported in the conclusions of a study of federal District Judges' decisions on the constitutionality of a Sentencing Reform Act.[69] Investigating the influence of social background, ideology, judicial role and institution and other factors on judges' decisions, the authors

[66] R.A. Posner, 'What do judges and justices maximize? (The same thing everybody else does)', *Supreme Court Economic Review*, 3 (1993), 1–41, 2.
[67] Ibid, p. 2.
[68] R.A. Posner, *How Judges Think*, Chapter 1.
[69] G. Sisk et al., 'Charting the influences on the judicial mind', p. 1499.

struggled to find convincing evidence of consistent demographic or ideological influences on outcome. They found some support for the legalist model of decision making and some evidence that background and attitudes influence decision making in some circumstances. But what struck them was the pleasure that judges appeared to take in writing and exercising analytical powers.

> In reading the many Sentencing Guidelines decisions, it was impossible not to be captivated by the excitement, the devotion to legal analysis, the depth and rigor of constitutional analysis, and, yes, the true pleasure revealed by the judges in their engagement with a meaningful legal problem.[70]

There is also an interesting *phenomenological* explanation of judicial behaviour that focuses on consciousness of being the judge. Posner, perhaps mischievously, argues that the pleasure of judging is bound up with compliance with certain self-limiting rules that define the role of judging. It might be a source of satisfaction to a judge to decide in favour of the litigant who irritates him, the lawyer who fails to show proper deference, or the side that represents a different social class from his own. For it is by doing such things that the judge knows that he is performing the judge role, not some other role. But this is, in fact, a serious issue, in particular in the lower courts where the judiciary are less in the public eye and where such a high proportion of decisions are discretionary, made rapidly and under time pressure.

[70] Ibid, p. 1499.

It has also been suggested that in order to understand fully why judges do what they do, it is necessary to think about the audiences for judicial behaviour and whose esteem they care about.[71] This is a controversial approach. Spock-like judges should have no interest in public approval. But economic theorists argue that judges care about approval from influential audiences because it has implications for career goals, for advancement and for effectiveness in legal policy making. A judge who wants an opportunity to 'do justice' – a chance to 'make a difference' – is making a statement about an interest in legal policy making. Why would judges' interests in approval not affect their choices? The core of the audience-based partial explanation of judicial behaviour is about self-presentation: people want to be liked and respected by others who are important to them; the desire to be liked and respected affects people's behaviour; in these respects, judges are people. Baum argues that understanding the influence of audience on judicial behaviour helps to fill in some of the motivational gaps in patterns of judicial behaviour. It may help to explain why judges are concerned with 'good' law or 'good' policy.

But what happens when there is no audience? When decisions are not written? When the public gallery is empty? Or when the determination is being made in chambers? What about the District Judge alone in court with two unrepresented parties and not even a clerk in the room? Who is the audience then? What are the operating factors on judicial behaviour? What does the judge fall back on? Legalistic adherence to

---

[71] L. Baum, *Judges and Their Audiences*, p. 22.

precedent? Pragmatic decision? His own sense of responsibility and ethical principles?

The work that has been done on developing theoretical models that help us to understand the range of influences on judicial decision making is interesting and important. There can be no doubt, even among the most committed legalists, that judges have a considerable degree of discretion and that in reaching their decisions they are not always and only applying legal rules. The studies conducted abroad to date suggest a complex mix of influences on judicial decisions both at the appellate and the trial level. In Britain, we have not even begun to explore these issues empirically. In a world of increasing pressures on the judiciary, enlarged discretion accompanied by decreased visibility and reviewability of judicial decisions, it is perhaps time to turn our attention to these issues. Are our judiciary 'genius saints', or 'all too human', or a mixture of both?

Research that examined preferences for one type of decision making rather than another would also provide insights into what attracts the judiciary into joining the bench. To ensure the judiciary continues to attract and motivate the most talented recruits it is important to understand the tasks and aspects of the judicial role that maintain judges' enthusiasm, and their intellectual and ethical commitment in the long term.[72]

---

[72] See the case of Sir Hugh Laddie, who was reported to have resigned from the High Court bench in 2006 because, among other things, he missed the collegiality of life at the Bar. Interview with Frances Gibb in *The Times*, 16 May 2006, http://business.timesonline.co.uk/tol/business/law/article717515.ece

Attractions of office

In common with most other aspects of the judicial role, we know little of why judges in the UK become judges.[73] But some clues have been obtained from a revealing small-scale study in which recently appointed High Court judges talked about their motivation for joining the bench and senior practitioners explained their interest in senior judicial appointment.[74] The explanations of what drew them away from practice and to the bench resonate with the mixture of motivations uncovered and hypothesised by political scientists and those legal scholars who have addressed the question of judicial behaviour and decision making – in particular the legalist and the pragmatic, but also some of the motivations suggested by economic models.

Recently appointed judges and senior practitioners interested in judicial appointment talked of the opportunity to make the decision; being in a position to 'do justice'; the opportunity to influence the development of the law; and the interest and intellectual challenge of the work on the High Court bench. These attractions suggest the dominance of legalist and pragmatic goals and also the appeal in the exercise of power.

> Intellectually the one thing I enjoyed as an arbitrator and still enjoy is actually working out the judgment. Not just making the decision, but coming up with the decision

---

[73] An exception is Penny Darbyshire's recent study. P. Darbyshire, 'Where do English and Welsh judges come from?', *Cambridge Law Journal*, 66: 2 (2007), 365–88.
[74] H. Genn, *The Attractiveness of Senior Judicial Appointment to Highly Qualified Practitioners* (Judicial Office for England, 2008).

and comprehensive reasons for what you are doing. It is intellectually challenging. Whatever kind of case. The decision has to be intellectually honest and stand up in logic. The intellectual stimulation is probably for me an important factor … As a judge, you are making decisions all the time. [High Court Judge]

In my experience of sitting part time at relatively low levels, you can do something you hope is the right thing in that case. You are not making earth-shattering developments of law, but you are making a real difference to a person's life. It is about doing the just thing. My longer-term aspiration is to contribute to the development of the law in a more general sense. I've thought quite carefully about it. I enjoy being a judge more than being an advocate, because ultimately as an advocate all I'm doing is making arguments for my clients. It is more satisfying intellectually and emotionally trying to do justice in a case. [QC]

It seems that practitioners with a strong commitment to legal policy making may eventually become frustrated by the advocacy role which is, in the end, that of a bystander as far as the development of the law is concerned. Crossing to the bench offers the opportunity to relieve those frustrations and to exercise the power to shape the law.

Being a full-time judge gives you the opportunity to shape the law. Actually to do things according to what you think the law *should* be rather than when representing clients saying what the law should be to suit your client. I like the law. [High Court Judge]

I do find making the decision very interesting, but sometimes I think, 'My goodness! I've got to make a decision.' It is interesting to be able to evaluate arguments

168

on either side. Advocacy requires completely different skills. For most people who spend their lives advocating, it is an advantage to be the person making the decision. [QC]

But the same judges also talked of the prestige of the appointment and the fact that it signified professional acknowledgement of excellence within the profession. Of having arrived at the top and being recognised as an outstanding lawyer. This clearly signals the importance of audience and presumably a desire to retain that high opinion.

> To become a judge – I'm not talking about the status and the knighthood – but you are seen as a serious player in the legal world. I am genuinely interested in the law and I thought it would be interesting to actually make the decisions. And there is an element of public service. If I continued at the Bar to sixty-five after forty years and retired having made a lot of money, I might have looked back and thought that rather selfish. It is stimulating. I am pleased to be doing it. So far so good. [High Court Judge]

However, some judges and practitioners were frank enough to say that they saw the bench as a 'safe haven' – a relief from the stress of practice and offering the promise of financial security. Perhaps judges with these kinds of motivations are less likely to be policy shapers and more likely to deliver 'go-along' decisions. For others, the bench was an opportunity for altruism and for public service after years of profitable practice.

An interesting factor both in motivating practitioners to join the bench and inhibiting them from doing so was the issue of temperament. People referred to being *temperamentally suited* to the bench or *temperamentally unsuited* to the Bar. The bench was seen as requiring the qualities of self-discipline, responsibility and *silence* as compared with the gregarious and sometimes raucous life at the Bar.

> Some people are cut out to be advocates and some are cut out to act judicially. It is a different set of skills. There is also a personality side to it. Some advocates don't want to be the judge because they are too lively. Many advocates like a crowd; they are very extrovert, very clubbable. Many are magnificent at what they do. I wasn't ever the most extrovert type. Those people would wither as judges. You spend a lot of time alone in your room or in court. At the end of the case, you spend a lot of time working it out on your own. Here people are friendly, but not clubbable. Temperamentally some would regard the judicial life as lonely. They don't like the responsible, reflective side. As advocates, they can have fun and try it on – be irresponsible. As a judge, you have to behave yourself and be responsible and dependable. You can see that different personalities are better at one than the other. Some people would never be attracted to judicial office. [High Court Judge]
>
> Judicial office was always on my horizon. I felt I was born to do it. To hear both sides of a case and come to a decision. I enjoy the procedure of ensuring a fair hearing and I enjoy the responsibility of deciding. I have the temperament to do it. I am pretty equable. You have got to be capable of being open-minded. Not forming judgements too quickly is also a challenge. [High Court Judge]

Some advocates positively feel that their personality is poorly suited to judicial office and this includes some high-flying Silks who had declined appointment to the High Court bench after being 'tapped on the shoulder' by a Lord Chancellor. They feel that the judicial role required a sense of responsibility and steadiness which they might find difficult to project full time.

> It's a very jolly life not being a judge. Getting loads of money, making jokes and doing really interesting work. You do really unusual, fascinating things working with people you like. There is lots of flexibility, long holidays, no bureaucracy. Why would you stop? [QC]
>
> I am not sure I would be a good judge. I think the skills I bring are suited to adversarial work. I am not sure that is the same as being interested in a just and correct conclusion. Being fair and just is extremely tiring. I have a very focused function as an advocate. I don't have to worry. I have a much narrower area of concern. [QC]
>
> Being a full-time judge wouldn't appeal to me. The main reason is that I enjoy the advocacy. Being on my hind legs and interfering with people. If I am honest, it's actually less difficult being the person who doesn't actually decide the outcome. I am not sure that decision making is in my character. I am not sure I like sitting in judgement on people. That role is not why I came into law. I didn't want to decide the final outcome. I prefer explaining all avenues. I would be going away wondering if I had misunderstood or made a wrong decision. [QC]
>
> I don't think that really good advocates make good judges. They take a partisan view. Fighting for clients all the way. They don't easily throw off that approach once they put on a judge's gown … The ones who are better suited to the Bench are those who spend time in chambers thinking

about legal problems and writing. Giving advice on complex legal problems. That's why the quality of the judges in the Chancery Bar is pretty high … The Chancery Bench is very aloof. It is difficult to appear before them. They are very tightly curled. From another planet. [QC]

Temperament clearly is important on the bench and the responses of interviewees raises questions about the extent to which different people with different temperaments seek judicial office. Which temperaments are best suited to judicial office and do the demands of the solitary, rarefied atmosphere of the High Court bench demand a different temperament from the demands of the Circuit and District benches? How do different temperaments map, if at all, on to judicial style and decision making? And what are the factors that determine how decisions are made in the rough and tumble of the lower civil courts? The answer is that we don't really know and have yet to begin to develop empirically based theoretical models that would help us to understand decision-making processes in the judicial trenches.[75]

Changed expectations of the judiciary in civil justice

Accepting the huge differences between judges at different levels in the judicial hierarchy, it is clear that the

---

[75] The tentative steps taken by a few empirical legal scholars in this direction have involved the concept of 'craft' to help understand and evaluate the work of judges. Kritzer in his article on judgecraft ('Toward a theorization of judgecraft') suggests that elements in the concept of 'craft' – such as consistency, skills and techniques and problem solving – are all essential aspects of judicial work.

reforms of civil justice, together with resource pressures, have fundamentally changed the nature of the judicial role. These changes are probably greatest below the High Court and are visible around the world in the wake of the civil justice reviews discussed in Chapter 2.[76] The post-Woolf judge in the civil courts is an active case manager rather than a remote and passive umpire.[77] The new Civil Procedure Rules make clear that the overriding objective of 'doing justice' in the civil courts requires the judge to balance values of efficiency, equality, expedition, proportionality and careful allocation of the scarce resources of the court.[78] Active case management includes encouraging co-operation between the parties; early identification of issues and summary disposal of as many issues as possible; encouraging, facilitating and, indeed, directing the use of ADR; helping the parties to settle the whole or part of the case; fixing timetables; considering the costs and benefits of taking procedural steps in the case; disposing of issues at the same time when possible; making use of technology and dealing with parties remotely if possible; and making directions to ensure that the case

---

[76] See for example Justice R. Sackville, 'From access to justice to managing justice: the transformation of the judicial role', Australian Institute of Judicial Administration Annual Conference, 'Access to justice – the way forward', Brisbane, Queensland (12–14 July 2002): 'While the core functions discharged by the judiciary remain intact, the manner in which those functions are discharged has been transformed. Moreover, the transformation has occurred over a very brief period of time ... The most obvious and frequently noticed change is that Australian courts now actively manage their caseloads.'

[77] Lord Woolf, *The Pursuit of Justice*, Chapter 10, p. 175.

[78] CPR R1.4(1).

proceeds quickly and efficiently.[79] One might be forgiven for thinking that the performance of the judiciary is evaluated more by reference to how they administer an efficient system rather than on substantive outcomes.

Critics of managerial judging, particularly in the USA, have suggested that judicial efforts to reduce costs may have the opposite effect and that emphasis on efficient case processing may result in litigation outcomes that are less fair or accurate.[80] It is also argued that wide discretion in case management decisions leads to inconsistency, which may threaten procedural fairness.[81] Resnik argues that over the last sixty years in the USA, the pre-trial stage in legal proceedings has ceased to be a prelude to trial but instead is presumed to lead to the conclusion of cases.[82] In a context in which judges are expected to make deals, settle and promote ADR, proceeding to trial represents a failure of the system.[83] She suggests that as the judiciary rush to process mountains of work, no one is assessing whether expecting trial judges to undertake informal dispute resolution and case management, either before or after trial, is good, bad or neutral. There is little empirical evidence to support the claim that judicial management 'works' either to settle cases or to provide cheaper, quicker or fairer dispositions. Resnik

[79] CPR R1.4 (2) (a)–(l).
[80] Michael Zander has also argued trenchantly that managerial judging increases legal costs, M. Zander, *The State of Justice*, pp. 44–5.
[81] J.T. Molot, 'An old judicial role for a new litigation era', *Yale Law Journal*, 113 (2003), 27–118.
[82] J. Resnik, 'Trial as error, jurisdiction as injury: transforming the meaning of Article III', *Harvard Law Review*, 113 (2000), 924–1038, 937.
[83] Ibid, p. 937.

also argues that there has been no evaluation of the systemic effects of this change in the judicial role; in particular how low-visibility managerial decision making gives more power to the lower courts judging and fewer protections to litigants. '[M]anagerial judging may be redefining sub silentio our standards of what constitutes rational, fair, and impartial adjudication.'[84]

In England the size of the judiciary at the lower levels has grown in recent years to accommodate the increase in caseload of the county courts as work has been pushed down the judicial hierarchy.[85] District judges who are at the base of the civil judicial hierarchy deal with an enormously wide range of cases. Much of this work is out of the courtroom, in chambers and out of public view. Moreover, cases are often disposed of without the benefit of legal representation on either side. Thus the District Judge has no assistance from representatives in understanding the issues in the case and in disposing of the case, the judge's conduct and decision making are not subjected to professional scrutiny. The following

---

[84] Ibid, p. 980.

[85] The Courts and Legal Services Act 1990 produced a significant reallocation of cases from the High Court to the county courts by enlarging the jurisdiction of the county courts. In raising the limit on small claims and allocating cases to procedural tracks, the Civil Procedure Rules have continued that downward movement of cases. Judicial statistics for the year ending 1999 report the numbers of Circuit Judges as 553, Recorders as 907, Assistant Recorders as 446 and District Judges as 383. Judicial statistics for the year ending 2008 show that the numbers were then as follows: Circuit Judges 653, Recorders 1,305, District Judges 438 and Deputy District Judges 773.

is an account of the challenges of life on the bench given by a
Deputy District Judge:

> The full range of DJ work includes all manner of civil
> disputes from small claims and disputes about poor
> workmanship/repair, e.g. fitting kitchens/bathrooms
> etc. etc., to consumer credit complaints, personal injury,
> insolvency, enforcement of debts/orders, bankruptcy,
> housing, landlord and tenant, disputes between
> neighbours, family cases involving money (ancillary
> relief), children, divorce, domestic violence … the list
> goes on and on. They range from pretty straightforward
> contractual disputes or low-level personal injury to very
> complex contractual disputes, serious money on ancillary
> relief. It is difficult to know how complicated until you
> get right into the case because often they will be poorly
> pleaded by people without the benefit of advice.

Although one might argue that our normative
expectations of the judiciary in terms of competence, independence, impartiality and fairness apply to judges at all
levels in the hierarchy, how in practice do they translate in
the real world of the lower courts? For example, in conversation recently a distinguished QC remarked on his admira-
tion for District Judges. Having attended a Judicial Studies
Board training course, he was dumbstruck at the complexity of property issues that District Judges face and have to
resolve under extreme time pressures. He felt that District
Judges in the county courts regularly grapple with issues
that in the Chancery Division would be considered worthy
of three days of legal argument. Nonetheless, because they

affect the affairs of those on low incomes, the issues must be sorted out quickly.

The reality of the pressures on the judiciary in the lower courts is well described by the recent appointee talking about her approach to managing her lists:

> The length of time for each case is very variable depending on the type of list. In a possession list last Friday I had forty-two cases listed all at the same time with a time allocation of five minutes. I find that even if people don't turn up, it takes more than five minutes to look at something meaningfully. People now turn up more frequently to protect their home. Then it takes much longer and it's very stressful. Often it doesn't really justify re-listing because there is no real defence, but of course the person wants to tell you all about it. It is a real struggle in those situations not to say, 'Look, I've got five minutes and there are twenty-five others waiting outside.' Instead you try and listen to a bit of what they have to say and gently point out what is and is not relevant: the tension between doing justice/being seen to be fair and the nature/length of the lists is often just terrible.

What, then, are the expectations in terms of standards of fairness and expertise at this level? How do they differ from what we expect in the High Court? And what impact does judicial behaviour in the high volume of cases at the lowest end of the judicial system have on public confidence in the judiciary and the legitimacy of the judiciary as an institution? At the lower levels with fewer obvious constraints and audiences, is there a need for a greater emphasis on self-aware, reflective judges with significant self-discipline? It is here that the 'phenomenological' approach to judicial decision making might be essential. Out of the public eye, with limited representation and significant time pressures one might think that the judiciary require more awareness of acting 'as a judge' with all of the legal, moral and ethical imperatives. In the absence of empirical data about how the judiciary *do justice* it is difficult to provide a convincing answer to such questions. However, the level of commitment and sense of duty shown by the judiciary in the difficult circumstances of the civil courts was brought home to me in an extraordinary scene one Friday afternoon when I had been spending a day with a judge. The judge was faced with a litigant in person who was haranguing him about various issues to do with his living arrangements. The man clearly had special needs. There was no clerk available to assist. The judge did not want to leave the situation over the weekend. He retired to his chambers and started telephoning around the local social services departments to see whether he could locate a social worker to help out. He would not leave the man in difficulties and could not himself go home until he had personally sorted out the case. He was still there telephoning when I left.

Conclusion

At all levels in the hierarchy, judges are responsible for decisions of immediate and direct impact on the lives of ordinary citizens. We need, expect and often heroically receive high standards of intellect, commitment and humanity applied to judicial decisions. But I would argue that at the lower levels – where the disputes, troubles and rights of the less powerful, less well resourced and less knowledgeable citizens are determined – the pressures and burden of delivering that service require a different kind of effort and are under a different kind of strain.

Our lack of understanding of the reality of judicial work, both at the higher levels and in the trenches, limits our ability to specify more precisely what it takes to be a good judge – other than that we know that we need them to be very good. But it would be helpful to have a more detailed understanding of the role of the judge in the real world and, in selecting on merit, to have greater clarity about what it is that we need judges to be able to do well and how we go about collecting evidence about their ability to do that.

A better understanding of the reality of judges' work would assist in articulating with greater precision the critical skills, attitudes and values that constitute excellence in the judicial role, not only from the perception of fellow judges or the profession (the natural 'audience' for the judiciary) but from the perspective of private citizens and business disputants who choose to bring their cases to the courts for determination. We might learn what judicial styles are most effective in promoting confidence and perceptions of fairness. This is important for the authority and legitimacy of the judiciary. Studying how justice is done might reveal areas of strain within the court system. If corrosion of public confidence is a genuine threat (about which we have no idea), it would assist in shoring up those areas of activity that would best halt decline in confidence or promote renewed confidence. We might also ask ourselves whether the reduction in the issue of proceedings and trials, and the drift into private dispute resolution, is, in fact, a socially positive development – a healthy sign of early settlement, or an unhealthy sign of diminishing confidence in the courts.

Finally, with growing numbers of applicants for judicial office, it is even more important to understand the skills necessary for outstanding performance. In a profession where appointment effectively means appointment for life, are we clear enough about who the supreme exponents of professional judging are? Would we be able to describe in detail, to analyse those characteristics and thus refine our selection processes? The Judicial Appointments Commission is responsible for making appointments of critical social and constitutional importance. It is recruiting to the third arm of government – not by election but by selection. The JAC therefore acts on behalf of society, not government. It is identifying those who will enjoy life tenure, good remuneration and freedom from interference.

5

Conclusion

My starting and ending point in these lectures has been the belief that the machinery of civil justice sustains social stability and economic growth by providing public processes for resolving civil disputes, for enforcing legal rights and for protecting private and personal rights. I have argued that the civil courts contribute silently to social and economic well-being and that to a certain extent we have had the luxury of taking that for granted. Unlike citizens in other jurisdictions, while our preference may be to stay well away from the courts, their relative accessibility, their historically demanding procedures and incorrupt judiciary have provided a background sense of comfort. They have enabled citizens to feel that they live in an orderly society where, if the worst should happen, their rights could and would be protected through the system of justice.

I have also argued that we are witnessing the downgrading of that civil justice system. The degradation of the courts and starving of resources are symptoms of their declining significance to government. This development can be traced to the interaction and mutual reinforcement of a number of factors including, but not limited to, the following:

- escalating government expenditure on criminal prosecution, criminal defence and incarceration – all of which are paid for out of a single justice budget that must accommodate the needs of both criminal and civil justice;

181

- consequent pressure to contain expenditure wherever possible within the justice system;
- contradictory criticisms of the civil justice system that it facilitated too many claims and that it was procedurally elaborate and insufficiently accessible;
- an increasingly organised and professionalised legal profession successfully enforcing rights and creatively enlarging liabilities – and charging for those services; and
- the development of a new profession of mediators competing with the legal profession for its dispute-resolution work.

In these lectures I have suggested that the combined effect of these factors is that while the significance of the law and justice is daily reaffirmed in relation to criminal activity, discussion regarding civil justice has become dominated by anti-law, anti-adjudication rhetoric, and government policy has focused on cost saving and diversion of cases out of the courts. I have discussed the decline in the use of the civil courts and questioned whether this is a socially positive phenomenon. Is it evidence of the fact that, in common with some policy makers and judges, the public believes even a bad settlement is better than the best trial? Does it show that the public has heeded the warnings of Lord Woolf and other civil justice reformers and avoided the civil justice system, taking their disputes elsewhere or leaving them unresolved? Or is it a reflection of failure in the civil justice system and the abdication of State responsibility for providing accessible forums for peaceful dispute resolution? If it is a sign of the State withdrawing from civil justice, what are the implications for social and economic well-being?

I have argued that we need to develop and communicate more clearly, perhaps in terms that can easily be understood by the Treasury, a positive understanding of the role and value of the civil justice system. We need to articulate the principles that would help us to decide which cases require authoritative judicial determination and which cases we prefer to discourage, and we need to make clear the reasoning underlying these choices. I have also argued that because of its social and economic importance, the quality of our civil justice system should not be measured simply in terms of speed and cheapness, although a modern, efficient, customer-focused justice system should certainly be our aspiration and one that society deserves. Finally, I have argued that we need to re-establish civil justice as a public good, recognising that it has a significant social purpose that is as important to the health of society as criminal justice.

The need for empirical understanding

I would also argue that debate about and understanding of civil justice continues to be constrained by the lack of reliable empirical evidence about how its constituent parts operate and, indeed, bump against each other. During his Hamlyn Lecture – two decades ago – Sir Jack Jacob lamented the 'deplorable' fact that civil procedure is not a required subject in English law schools. He thought that in this respect England was unique and that a consequence was that civil procedure is the 'Cinderella' of the academic world. He argued that it is necessary to study what he called the micro features of civil justice – the principles governing the actual procedures and practices of the litigation and judicial processes – the 'law in action'. What was needed from academics in Sir Jack's view was research into civil justice, its past, its cultural and moral values and its social impacts, its defect and deficiencies and their remedies, its present operation and its prospects for the future in a critical, comparative and reformist spirit. 'They will create an improved climate of academic excellence in civil justice. They will not confine themselves to academic analysis but undertake field studies in different areas of the machinery of justice.'[1]

In these calls Sir Jack was echoing the sentiments of Bentham, who believed in the value of empirical evidence to inform procedural reform. Bentham believed that there was a need continually to test the system. Bentham's approach to reform was the empirical gathering of information, primarily in tables,[2] covering all relevant details from the number of cases commenced, to time taken in hearings and judgments, and the degree of movement of cases between courts in cases of appeal. Bentham carried out statistical comparisons between systems, courts and judges in order to provide a comprehensive empirical analysis and critique of civil procedure. Bentham apparently believed that if individual litigants could have access to this kind of information, they would be able to assess the progress of their cases and assess the effectiveness of the system of procedure. This would be

---

[1] Sir Jack Jacob, *The Fabric of English Civil Justice* (Sweet & Maxwell, 1987), pp. 252–4.
[2] A.J. Draper, 'Corruptions in the administration of justice: Bentham's critique of civil procedure, 1806–1811', *Journal of Bentham Studies*, 7 (2004).

empowering and would contribute to the effectiveness of the system.

Sir Jack also suggested that empirical research on civil justice should be interdisciplinary, conducted by lawyers closely co-operating 'with scholars in other social sciences and would seek to attract their interest and collaboration in the operation of civil justice. In every way, they would greatly enlarge, enrich and enhance the machinery of civil justice.'[3] But apparently losing this conviction, he later remarked:

> It is also important to remember that in searching for solutions to new problems in civil justice and in civil procedure especially, the constituency for consultation is generally very limited. It will ordinarily consist mainly of lawyers, judges and practitioners and probably the same judges and practitioners on one problem as on the next. Experts in other social sciences generally are not familiar enough with the technology of civil procedure to be really helpful and lawyers on the whole would regard their taking part in such enquiries with some questioning and doubt.[4]

In this respect, I believe that Sir Jack was quite wrong. At various moments in these lectures I have referred to the extent to which civil justice reforms have been devised and applied without prior investigation into the processes that are being regulated or any well-developed social, psychological and economic understanding of the dynamics of disputes and their resolution. We should not therefore be completely

---

[3] Sir Jack Jacob, *The Fabric of Civil Justice*, p. 254.
[4] Ibid, p. 284.

dumbfounded by the evidence that reforms do not always achieve their objectives. Lawyers, judges and practitioners do not necessarily have all of the answers. A decade ago, I argued strenuously about the urgent need for research into how the system of civil justice operates.[5] There is still no programme of research, no sustained commitment to evaluating the impact of changes, and no apparent appreciation of the need to collect data that would support good-quality policy evaluation. This is a dispiriting reflection of where the civil justice system sits in the priorities of government.

Postscript

When the Hamlyn Trustees kindly invited me to deliver the 2008 Hamlyn Lectures there was little doubt that I would focus on the civil justice system. Having spent most of my professional career hanging around courts and tribunals and involving myself in policy on the administration of justice it would have been surprising, if not perverse, to have chosen something less central to my interests. Moreover, there were a number of developments in civil justice that I felt quite strongly about, but had not had time to address on the treadmill of successive research projects. Indeed, I welcomed the opportunity to be able to stand back from the research data and reflect on some of these issues in the context of broader developments. At the end of my final lecture I said:

[5] H. Genn, 'Understanding civil justice', in M. Freeman (ed.), *Law and Public Opinion in the 20th Century*, Current Legal Problems Vol. 50 (Oxford University Press, 1997), p. 157.

I am grateful to the Hamlyn Trustees for giving me
the opportunity of these three lectures to make some
(possibly controversial) observations about civil justice
in England that have been troubling me for a while.
The main message, which I hope I have communicated,
is that we have a civil justice system of which we were
rightly proud and which, in my view, has been taken for
granted. We have neglected the importance of judicial
determination which has a critical function in our
common law civil justice system and an essential role in
supporting social and economic order. We continue to
expect our judiciary in the civil courts to perform to the
highest professional standards, but we do not provide the
resources or infrastructure to operate the modern and
efficient civil justice system that society needs. In taking
the importance of civil justice for granted, we have allowed
criminal justice to overwhelm justice discourse, policy and
spending. I think it is time to start redressing that balance.

Some months have passed since I delivered the lectures and in the intervening period, as a result of both oral
and written communications, I have realised, perhaps to a
much greater extent than at the time, first how controversial were some of my views and second how very strongly
those who agree with me and those who disagree with me
feel about the subject. Not wishing to over-dramatise what
is in the end a difference of view about means when everyone is pretty much agreed on the end, it is absolutely clear
that these are issues in need of some solid evidence and fresh
debate. It is also clear that the schism in opinion about what
the civil justice system should be doing and how it should

be operating is more pronounced than might appear from published material. If this book contributes constructively to debate and ultimately to a better understanding of why reform is so difficult, then it will have served a purpose that gives me satisfaction.

Abel, R.L., 'The contradictions of informal justice' in R.L. Abel (ed.), *The Politics of Informal Justice, Volume 1: The American Experience* (Academic Press, 1982).

Ackerman, R.M. 'Vanishing trial, vanishing community? The potential effect of the vanishing trial on America's social capital', *Journal of Dispute Resolution*, 7 (2006), 165–81.

Allan, J. 'Judicial appointments in New Zealand' in K. Malleson and P.H. Russell (eds), *Appointing Judges in An Age of Judicial Power* (University of Toronto Press, 2006), Chapter 5.

Allen, T., *A Closer Look at Halsey and Steel* (CEDR, 2004).

Andrews, N., *Principles of Civil Procedure* (Sweet and Maxwell, 1994).

Andrews, N., 'English civil justice and remedies, progress and challenges, Nagoya Lectures' (Nagoya University of Comparative Study of Civil Justice, 2007), Vol. I.

Attorney General Victoria, *Justice Statement* (Melbourne: Department of Justice, 2004).

Australian Government Productivity Commission, 'Justice', *Report on Government Services*, Vol. I, Part C (2008).

Australian Law Reform Commission, *Review of the Federal Civil Justice System*, Discussion Paper 62 (Sydney: ALRC, 1999).

Australian Law Reform Commission, *Managing Justice: A Review of the Federal Civil Justice System*, Report 89 (Sydney: ALRC, 2000).

Baldwin, J., *Small Claims in County Courts in England and Wales: The Bargain Basement of Civil Justice?* (Clarendon Press, 1997).

Baldwin, J., *Monitoring the Rise of the Small Claims Limit: Litigants' Experiences of Different Forms of Adjudication* (Lord Chancellor's Department, 1997).

Baldwin, J., 'Small claims hearings: the "interventionist" role played by district judges', *Civil Justice Quarterly* 17:1 (1998), 20–34.

189

Baldwin, J., *Lay and Judicial Perspectives on the Expansion of the Small Claims Regime* (Lord Chancellor's Department Research Series 8/02, 2002).

Barak, A., *The Judge in a Democracy* (Princeton University Press, 2006).

Baruch Bush, R.A. and Folger, J.P., *The Promise of Mediation: The Transformative Approach to Conflict* (Jossey-Bass, 2005).

Baum, L., *The Puzzle of Judicial Behavior* (University of Michigan Press, 1997).

Baum, L., *Judges and their Audiences* (Princeton University Press, 2006).

Bayles, M., 'Principles for legal procedure', *Law and Philosophy*, 5:1 (1986), 33–57.

Bell, J., *Judiciaries Within Europe: A Comparative Review* (Cambridge University Press, 2006).

Bernard, P.E. 'Minorities, mediation and method: the view from one court-connected mediation program', *Fordham Urban Law Journal*, 35:1 (January 2008).

Bingham, Lord, *The Business of Judging* (Oxford University Press, 2000).

Bingham, Lord, 'The rule of law', *Sixth David Williams Annual Lecture*, Centre for Public Law, Cambridge University (November 2006).

Blader, S. and Tyler, T.R., 'A four component model of procedural justice: defining the meaning of a "fair" process', *Personality and Social Psychology Bulletin*, 29 (2003), 747–58.

Bondy, V., Doyle, M. and Reid, V., 'Mediation and judicial review – mind the research gap', *Judicial Review* (September 2005).

Bondy, V. and Sunkin, M., 'Accessing judicial review', *Public Law* (Winter 2008), 647–67.

British Columbia Civil Justice Review Task Force, *Effective and Affordable Civil Justice*, (British Columbia Justice Review, November 2006).

Brooke, H., 'The future of civil justice, an address to the Civil Court Users Association', (26 March 2006).

Brooke, H., *Should the Civil Courts be Unified?* (Judicial Office, August 2008).

Brown, H. and Marriott, A., *ADR Principles and Practice*, 2nd edn (London: Sweet and Maxwell, 1999).

Buck, A., Pleasence, P. and Balmer, N., 'Do citizens know how to deal with legal issues? Some empirical insights', *Journal of Social Policy*, 37:4 (2008), 661–81.

Butler, P., 'The case for trials: considering the intangibles', *Journal of Empirical Legal Studies*, 1:3, (2004), 627–36.

Campbell, E. and Lee, H.P., *The Australian Judiciary* (Cambridge University Press, 2001).

Canadian Bar Association, *Task Force on Systems of Civil Justice* (Canadian Bar Association, 1996).

Canadian Forum on Civil Justice, *Public Perceptions of the Role of the Judiciary* (University of Alberta, 2005).

CEDR, *The CEDR Mediator Handbook: Effective Resolution of Commercial Disputes*, 4th edn (CEDR, 2004).

Civil Justice Reform Working Group, *Effective and Affordable Civil Justice* (Vancouver: Justice Review Task Force, 2006).

Conley, J.M. and O'Barr, W.M., 'Fundamentals of jurisprudence: an ethnography of judicial decision making in informal courts', *North Carolina Law Review*, 66 (1988), 467–508.

Coumarelos, C., Wei, Z. and Zhou, A., *Justice Made to Measure: NSW Legal Needs Survey in Disadvantaged Areas* (Law and Justice Foundation of New South Wales, Australia, 2006).

Couture, E.J., 'The nature of the judicial process', *Tulane Law Review*, 25 (1950), 1–28.

Cowan, D. and Hitchings, E., 'Pretty boring stuff': district judges and housing possession proceedings', *Social & Legal Studies*, 16:3 (2007), 363–82.

Cranston, R., *How Law Works: The Machinery and Impact of Civil Justice* (Oxford University Press, 2006).

Cross, F.B., 'Judicial partisanship and obedience to legal doctrine: whistleblowing on the Federal Courts of Appeals', *Yale Law Journal*, 107 (1998), 2155–76.

Cross, F.B., *Decision Making in the US Courts of Appeals* (Stanford University Press, 2007).

Damaska, M.R. *The Faces of Justice and State Authority* (Yale University Press, 1986).

Darbyshire, P. 'Where do English and Welsh judges come from?', *Cambridge Law Journal*, 66:2 (2007), 365–88.

Davies, G.L., 'Civil justice reform: why we need to question some basic assumptions', *Civil Justice Quarterly*, 25 (2006), 32–51.

Delgado, R. et al., 'Fairness and formality: minimizing the risk of prejudice in alternative dispute resolution', *Wisconsin Law Review* (1985), 1359.

Denning, Lord, *The Discipline of Law* (Oxford University Press, 1979).

Dhavan, R., Sudarshan, R. and Khurshid, S., *Judges and the Judicial Power: Essays in Honour of Justice V. R. Krishna Iyer* (Sweet and Maxwell, 1985).

Dingwall, R. and Cloatre, E., 'Vanishing trials?: An English perspective', *Journal of Dispute Resolution*, 7 (2006), 51–70.

Doyle, M., *Manchester Small Claims Mediation Scheme Evaluation* (Department for Constitutional Affairs, 2006).

Draper, A.J., 'Corruptions in the administration of justice: Bentham's Critique of Civil Procedure, 1806–1811', *Journal of Bentham Studies*, 7 (2004).

Eekelaar, J., 'Family justice: ideal or illusion? Family law and communitarian values' in M.D.A. Freeman (ed.), *Current Legal Problems* (Oxford University Press, 1996), pp. 161–216.

Ekman, P., *Telling Lies: Clues to Deceit in the Marketplace, Politics and Marriage* (W.W. Norton & Co, 2001).

Engel, D.M. and Steele, E.H., 'Civil cases and society: process and order in the civil justice system', *American Bar Foundation Research Journal* (1979), 295–346.

Enterken, J. and Sefton, M., *Evaluation of Reading Small Claims Mediation Scheme* (Department for Constitutional Affairs, 2006).

Epstein, L. (ed.), *Courts and Judges (The International Library of Essays in Law and Society)* (Ashgate, 2005).

Epstein, L. and Knight, J., *The Choices Justices Make* (C.Q. Press, 1998).

Feenan, D., 'Women judges: gendering judging, justifying diversity', *Journal of Law and Society*, 35:4 (2008), 490–519.

Feenan, D., 'Women and judging', *Feminist Legal Studies*, 17 (2009), 1–9.

Fenn, P., Rickman, N. and Vencappa, D., 'The impact of the Woolf Reforms on costs and delay' (Centre for Risk & Insurance Studies, 2009).

Fiss, O.M., 'Against settlement', *Yale Law Journal*, 93 (1984), 1073–90.

Fiss, O.M. and Resnik, J., *Adjudication and its Alternatives: An Introduction to Procedure* (Foundation Press, 2003).

Frank, J., *Courts on Trial, Myth and Beauty in American Justice* (Princeton University Press, 1949).

Friedman, L.M., *Total Justice* (Russell Sage Foundation, 1994).

Friedman, L.M., 'The day before trials vanished', *Journal of Empirical Legal Studies*, 1:3 (2004), 689–703.

Friedman Goldstein, L., 'From democracy to juristocracy', *Law and Society Review*, 38 (2004), 611–29.

Fuller, L.L., 'The forms and limits of adjudication', *Harvard Law Review*, 92 (1978), 353–408.

Further Findings: A Continuing Evaluation of the Civil Justice Reforms (Department for Constitutional Affairs, 2002).

Galanter, M., 'The radiating effects of courts' in K. Boyum and L. Mather (eds), *Empirical Theories About Courts* (New York, 1983).

Galanter, M., 'The vanishing trial: an examination of trials and related matters in federal and state courts', *Journal of Empirical Legal Studies*, 1:3 (2004), 459–570.

Galanter, M., *Lowering the Bar, Lawyer Jokes and Legal Culture* (University of Wisconsin Press, 2005).

Galanter, M., 'A world without trials', *Journal of Dispute Resolution*, 7 (2006), 7–34.

Galanter, M., 'In the winter of our discontent: law, anti–law and social science', *Annual Review of Law and Social Science*, 2 (2006), 1–16.

Garth, B., 'From civil litigation to private justice: legal practice at war with the profession and its values', *Brooklyn Law Review*, 59 (1993), 931–60.

Genn, H., 'Understanding civil justice' in M.D.A. Freeman (ed.), *Law and Public Opinion in the 20th Century*, Current Legal Problems Vol. 50 (Oxford University Press, 1997).

Genn, H., *Central London Pilot Mediation Scheme, Evaluation Report* (Department for Constitutional Affairs, 1998).

Genn, H., *Paths to Justice: What People Think and Do About Going to Law* (Hart Publishing, 1999).

Genn, H., *Court Based ADR Initiatives for Non-Family Civil Cases* (Department for Constitutional Affairs, Research series 1/02, 2002).

Genn, H., *The Pre-Woolf Litigation Landscape in the County Courts* (September 2002), www.ucl.ac.uk/laws/genn.

Genn, H., *Solving Civil Justice Problems: What Might Be Best* (Scottish Consumer Council Seminar on Civil Justice, January 2005), www.ucl.ac.uk/laws/genn.

Genn, H., *The Attractiveness of Senior Judicial Appointment to Highly Qualified Practitioners* (Judicial Office for England, December 2008).

Genn, H. et al., *Tribunals for Diverse Users* (London: Department for Constitutional Affairs, Research Series 1/06, 2006).

Genn, H. et al., *Twisting Arms: Court Referred and Court Linked Mediation Under Judicial Pressure* (Ministry of Justice Research Series 1/07, 2007).

Genn, H. and Genn, Y., *Representation in Tribunals* (Lord Chancellor's Department, 1989).

Glendon, M.A., *A Nation Under Lawyers* (Harvard University Press, 1996).

Goode, R., *Commercial Law in the Next Millennium*, 49th Hamlyn Lectures (Sweet and Maxwell, 1998).

Gramatikov, M., 'Multiple Justiciable Problems in Bulgaria', Tilburg University Legal Studies Working Paper No. 16/2008 (2008).

Grillo, T., 'The mediation alternative: process dangers for women', *Yale Law Journal*, 100:6 (1991), 1545–610.

Guarneri, C. and Pederzoli, P., *From Democracy to Juristocracy? The Power of Judges: A Comparative Study of Courts and Democracy* (Oxford University Press, 2002).

Guthrie, C., Rachlinski, J.J. and Wistrich, A.J., 'Inside the judicial mind', *Cornell Law Review*, 86 (2001), 777.

Guthrie, C., Rachlinski, J.J. and Wistrich, A.J., 'Blinking on the bench: how judges decide cases', *Cornell Law Review*, 93 (2007), 1–43.

Hadfield, G.K., 'Where have all the trials gone? Settlement, non-trial adjudications, and statistical artifacts in the changing disposition of federal civil cases', *Journal of Empirical Legal Studies*, 1:3 (2004), 705–34.

Hale, B., 'Equality and the judiciary: why should we want more women judges?', *Public Law* (2001), 489.

Hann, R.G. and Baar, C., *Evaluation of the Ontario Mandatory Mediation Program (Rule 24.1): Final Report – The First 23 Months*, (Ontario Ministry of the Attorney General, March 2001).

Hanycz, C.M., 'Through the looking glass: mediator conceptions of philosophy, process and power', *Alberta Law Review*, 42 (2004–5), 819–85.

Hanycz, C.M., 'More access to less justice: efficiency, proportionality and costs in Canadian civil justice reform', *Civil Justice Quarterly*, 27:1 (2008), 98–122.

Hensler, D.R., 'Suppose it's not true: challenging mediation ideology', *Journal of Dispute Resolution* (2002), 81–100.

Hensler, D.R., 'Our courts, ourselves: how the alternative dispute resolution movement is re-shaping our legal system', *Penn State Law Review*, 108 (2003), 167–97.

Higginbotham, P.E., 'So why do we call them trial courts?', *Southern Methodist University Law Review*, 55 (2002), 1405–21.

Hirschl, R., *Towards Juristocracy: The Origins and Consequences of the New Constitutionalism* (Harvard University Press, 2004).

Hirschl, R., 'Juristocracy – political, not juridical', *The Good Society*, 13:3 (2004), 6–11.

Hollander-Blumoff, R. and Tyler, T.R., 'Procedural justice in negotiation: procedural fairness, outcome acceptance, and integrative potential', *Law and Social Inquiry*, 33:2 (2008), 473–500.

Hong Kong Department of Justice, *Consultancy Study on the Demand for and Supply of Legal and Related Services* (Hong Kong Department of Justice, 2008).

Hong Kong Judiciary, *Reform of the Civil Justice System in Hong Kong*, Final Report of the Working Party on Civil Justice Reform (Hong Kong Judiciary, 2004).

House of Commons Constitutional Affairs Committee, 'Civil legal aid: adequacy of provision', *Conclusions and Recommendations* (Fourth Report of Session 2003–04), Vol. I, HC 391–I.

Hyman, J.M. and Love, L.P., 'If Portia were a mediator: an inquiry into justice in mediation', *Clinical Law Review*, 9 (2002), 157.

Jackson, Lord Justice, *Civil Litigation Costs Review, Preliminary Report* (Judicial Office, 8 May 2009).

Jacob, Sir J., 'The reform of civil procedural law', reprinted in *The Reform of Civil Procedural Law and Other Essays in Civil Procedure* (Sweet and Maxwell, 1982).

Jacob, Sir J., *The Fabric of English Civil Justice* (Sweet and Maxwell, 1987).

Jacob, J.M., *Civil Justice in the Age of Human Rights* (Ashgate, 2007).

Jacobs, Sir J., 'Access to justice in England' in M. Cappelletti and B. Garth (eds), *Access to Justice, Vol 1: a World Survey* (Alphen aan den Rhijn/Milan, 1978).

Jolowicz, J.A., *On Civil Procedure* (Cambridge University Press, 2000).

Justice for All, White Paper (The Stationery Office, 2002), CM 5563.

Kenney, S.J., 'Gender on the agenda: how the paucity of women judges became an issue', *Journal of Politics*, 70:3 (2008), 717–35.

Kirby, M., *Judicial Activism: Authority, Principle and Policy in the Judicial Method*, The Hamlyn Lectures 55th Series (Sweet and Maxwell, 2004).

Kleinig, J., 'Judicial corrosion: outlines of a theory', Conference on *Confidence in the Judiciary* (Canberra, February 2007).

Kritzer, H.M., 'Disappearing trials? A comparative perspective', *Journal of Empirical Legal Studies*, 1:3 (2004), 735–54.

Kritzer, H.M., 'Towards a theorization of judgecraft', *Social & Legal Studies*, 16:3 (2007), 321–40.

Lacey, N., *The Prisoner's Dilemma*, The Hamlyn Lectures 59th Series (Cambridge University Press, 2008).

LaFree, G. and Rack, C., 'The effects of participants' ethnicity and gender on monetary outcomes in mediated and adjudicated civil cases', *Law and Society Review*, 30 (1996), 767–94.

Lande, J., 'How much justice can we afford? Defining the courts' roles and deciding the appropriate number of trials, settlement signals, and other elements needed to administer justice', *Journal of Dispute Resolution* (2006), 213.

Landsman, S., 'So what? Possible implications of the vanishing trial phenomenon', *Journal of Empirical Legal Studies*, 1:3 (2004), 973–84.

Legal Services Consultation Document, *A New Focus For Civil Legal Aid: Encouraging Early Resolution; Discouraging Unnecessary Litigation* (Department for Constitutional Affairs, 2004).

Leubsdorf, J., 'The myth of civil procedure reform' in A.A.S. Zuckerman (ed.), *Civil Justice in Crisis: Comparative Aspects of Civil Procedure* (Oxford University Press, 1999), Chapter 2.

Lind, E.A. and Tyler, T.R., *The Social Psychology of Procedural Justice* (Plenum, 1988).

Lines, M., 'Empirical study of civil justice systems: a look at the literature', *Alberta Law Review*, 42:3 (2005), 887–905.

Luban, D., *Lawyers and Justice* (Princeton University Press, 1988), p. 251.

Luban, D., 'Settlements and the erosion of the public realm', *Georgetown Law Review*, 83 (1995), 2638.

Mack, K. and Roach Anleu, S., 'Getting through the list: judgecraft and legitimacy in the lower courts', *Social & Legal Studies*, 16 (2007), 341–61.

Mackie, K., Miles, D., Marsh, W. and Allen, T., *The ADR Practice Guide: Commercial Dispute Resolution*, 3rd revised edition (Tottel Publishing, 2007).

Malleson, K., *The New Judiciary: The Effects of Expansion and Activism* (Ashgate Press, 1999).

Manning, K.L., Carroll, B.A. and Carp, R.A., 'Does age matter? Judicial decision making in age discrimination cases', *Social Science Quarterly*, 85:1 (March 2004), 1–18.

Marcus, R.L., 'Malaise of the litigation superpower' in A.A.S. Zuckerman, *Civil Justice in Crisis, Comparative Perspectives of Litigation Procedure* (Oxford University Press, 1999), Chapter 3.

Mautner, M., 'Luck in the courts', *Theoretical Inquiries in Law*, 9 (2008), 217–38.

McEwan, J., *The Verdict of the Court, Passing Judgment in Law and Psychology* (Hart Publishing, 2003).

McNeill, D., *The Face* (Hamish Hamilton, 1998).

Megarry, R.E., *Lawyer and Litigant in England*, The Hamlyn Lectures 14th Series (Stevens, 1962).

Memon, A., Vrij, A. and Bull, R., *Psychology and Law: Truthfulness, Accuracy and Credibility*, 2nd edn (John Wiley, 2003).

Menkel-Meadow, C., 'The many ways of mediation: the transformation of tradition, ideologies, paradigms and practices', *Negotiation Journal*, 11 (1995), 217–42.

Menkel-Meadow, C., 'Whose dispute is it anyway? A philosophical and democratic defense of settlement (in some cases)', *Georgetown Law Journal*, 83 (1995), 2663–96.

Menkel-Meadow, C., 'The trouble with the adversary system in a postmodern, multicultural world', *William and Mary Law Review*, 38 (1996), 5–44.

Menkel-Meadow, C., 'Ethics in Alternative dispute resolution: new issues, no answers from the adversary conception of lawyers' responsibilities', *South Texas Law Review*, 38:2 (1997), 407–54.

Menkel-Meadow, C., 'Mothers and fathers of invention: the intellectual founders of ADR', *Ohio State Journal on Dispute Resolution*, 16:1 (2000), 1–37.

Menkel-Meadow, C. (ed.), *Mediation: Theory, Policy and Practice* (Ashgate, 2001).

Menkel-Meadow, C., 'Peace and justice: notes on the evolution and purposes of legal processes', *Georgetown Law Journal*, 94 (2006), 553–80.

Mnookin, R.H. and Kornhauser, L., 'Bargaining in the shadow of the law: the case of divorce', *Yale Law Journal*, 88 (1979), 950–97.

Molot, J.T., 'An old judicial role for a new litigation era', *Yale Law Journal*, 113 (2003), 27–118.

Moorhead, R. and Cowan, D., 'Judgecraft: an introduction', *Social & Legal Studies*, 16:3 (2007), 315–20.

Moorhead, R. and Sefton, M., *Litigants in Person: Unrepresented Litigants in First Instance Proceedings* (Department for Constitutional Affairs, Research Series, 2005).

Moorhead, R., Sefton, M. and Scanlan, L., *Just Satisfaction? What Drives Public and Participant Satisfaction with Courts and Tribunals* (Ministry of Justice, Research Series 5/08, 2008).

Mulcahy, L., 'The possibilities and desirability of mediator neutrality – towards an ethics of partiality?', *Social & Legal Studies*, 10:4 (2001), 505–27.

Murayama, M., 'Experiences of problems and disputing behaviour in Japan', *Meiji Law Journal*, 14 (2007), 1–59.

Niemeijer, B. and Pel, M., 'Court-based mediation in the Netherlands: research, evaluation and future expectations', *Penn State Law Review*, 110:2 (2005), 345–79.

Nolan-Haley, J.M., 'Court mediation and the search for justice through law', *Washington University Law Quarterly* (January 1996), 49.

Olson, S.M. and Huth, D.A., 'Explaining public attitudes toward local courts', *Justice System Journal*, 20 (1998), 41.

Paterson, A.A. and Goriely, T., *A Reader on Resourcing Civil Justice*, Oxford Readings in Socio-Legal Studies (Oxford University Press, 1996).

Pleasence, P., Balmer, N.J., Tam, T., Buck, A., Smith, M. and Patel, A., *Civil Justice in England and Wales: Report of the 2007 English and Welsh Civil and Social Justice Survey* (Legal Services Commission, 2008), LSRC Research Paper No. 22.

Pleasence, P., Buck, A., Balmer, N., Genn, H., O'Grady, A. and Smith, M., *Causes of Action: Civil Law and Social Justice* (The Stationery Office, 2004).

Posner, R.A., 'What do judges and justices maximize? (The same thing everybody else does)', *Supreme Court Economic Review*, 3 (1993), 1–41.

Posner, R.A., *How Judges Think* (Harvard University Press, 2008).

Prince, S., *Evaluation of Exeter Small Claims Mediation Scheme* (Department for Constitutional Affairs, 2006).

Prince, S., 'ADR after the CPR' in D. Dwyer (ed.), *The Civil Procedure Rules Ten Years On* (Oxford University Press, 2009).

Prince, S. and Belcher, S., *An Evaluation of the Effectiveness of Court-based Mediation Processes in Non-Family Civil Proceedings at Exeter and Guildford County Courts* (Department for Constitutional Affairs, 2006).

Radcliffe, Lord, *Not in Feather Beds* (Hamish Hamilton, 1968).

Reid, Lord, *The Law and the Reasonable Man* (Proceedings of the British Academy, 1968).

Resnik, J., 'Managerial judges', *Harvard Law Review*, 96 (1982), 374–446.

Resnik, J., 'Many doors? Closing doors? Alternative dispute resolution and adjudication', *Ohio State Journal on Dispute Resolution*, 10:2 (1995), 211–65.

Resnik, J., 'Trial as error, jurisdiction as injury: transforming the meaning of Article III', *Harvard Law Review*, 113 (2000), 924–1038.

Resnik, J., 'Mediating preferences: litigant preferences for process and judicial preferences for settlement', *Journal of Dispute Resolution* (2002), 155–69.

Resnik, J., 'Migrating, morphing, and vanishing: the empirical and normative puzzles of declining trial rates in courts', *Journal of Empirical Legal Studies*, 1:3 (2004), 783–841.

Resnik, J., 'Courts: in and out of sight, site and cite', *Villanova Law Review*, 53 (2008), 771–810.

Resnik, J. and Curtis, D., 'Representing justice: from Renaissance iconography to twenty-first century courthouses', *Proceedings of the American Philosophical Society*, 151 (2007), 139.

Roach Anleu, S. and Mack, K., 'Magistrates' everyday work and emotional labour', *Journal of Law and Society*, 32:4 (2005), 590–614.

Robertson, D., *Judicial Discretion in the House of Lords* (Oxford University Press, 1998).

Rottman, D.B., *Public Trust and Confidence in the State Courts: A Primer*, National Center for State Courts, Working Paper (March 1999).

Sackville, Justice R., 'From access to justice to managing justice: the transformation of the judicial role', Australian Institute of Judicial Administration Annual Conference, 'Access to Justice – The Way Forward', Brisbane, Queensland (12–14 July 2002).

Sallmann, P. A. and Wright, R.T., *Going to Court: A Discussion Paper on Civil Justice in Victoria*, Civil Justice Review Project (Victoria Department of Justice, 2000).

Sandefur, R.L., 'Access to civil justice and race, class, and gender inequality', *Annual Review of Sociology*, 34 (2008), 339–58.

Scott, K.E., 'Two models of the civil process', *Stanford Law Review*, 27:3 (1975), 937–50.

Sherry, S., 'Civil virtue and the feminine voice in constitutional adjudication', *Virginia Law Review*, 72 (1986), 543–616.

Sisk, G.C., 'The quantitative moment and the qualitative opportunity: legal studies of judicial decision making' (book review), *Cornell Law Review*, 93:2 (2008), 873.

Sisk, G.C. and Heise, M., 'Judges and ideology: public and academic debates about statistical measures', *Northwestern University Law Review*, 99 (2005), 743.

Sisk, G.C., Heise, M. and Morriss, A.P., 'Charting the influences on the judicial mind: an empirical study of judicial reasoning', *New York University Law Review*, 73 (1998), 1377–500.

Sisk, G.C., Heise, M. and Morriss, A.P., 'Searching for the soul of judicial decision making: an empirical study of religious freedom decisions', *Ohio State Law Journal*, 65:3 (2004), 491.

Smith, R. (ed.), *Achieving Civil Justice: Appropriate Dispute Resolution for the 1990s* (Legal Action Group, 1996).

Solum, L.B., 'Procedural justice', *Southern California Law Review*, 78 (2004), 181.

Stipanowick, T.J., 'ADR and the 'vanishing trial': the growth and impact of alternative dispute resolution', *Journal of Empirical Legal Studies*, 1:3 (2004), 843–912.

Strasser, F. and Randolph, P., *Mediation: A Psychological Insight into Conflict Resolution* (Continuum, 2004).

Stratton, M., 'Public perceptions of the role of the Canadian judiciary', *The Canadian Forum on Civil Justice* (December 2005).

Stulberg, J.B., 'Mediation and justice: what standards govern?' *Cardozo Journal of Conflict Resolution*, 6 (2005), 213–45.

Sun, I.Y. and Wu, Y., 'Citizens' perceptions of the courts: the impact of race, gender and recent experience', *Journal of Criminal Justice*, 34 (2006), 457–67.

Susskind, R., *The End of Lawyers: Rethinking the Nature of Legal Services* (Oxford University Press, 2008).

Tamanaha, B., *On The Rule of Law: History, Politics, Theory* (Cambridge University Press, 2004).

Thomas, Lord Justice, Senior Presiding Judge of England and Wales, *The Maintenance of Local Justice*, The Sir Elwyn Jones Memorial Lecture (Bangor University, October 2004).

Van de Walle, S. and Raine, J.W., *Explaining Attitudes Towards the Justice System in the UK and Europe* (Ministry of Justice Research Series 9/08, 2008).

Victorian Law Reform Commission, *Civil Justice Review, Report 14* (Victorian Law Reform Commission, 28 May 2008).

Voight, S. 'Economic growth, certainty in the law and judicial independence' in Transparency International, *Global Corruption Report 2007: Corruption in Judicial Systems* (Cambridge University Press, 2007).

Vrij, A., *Detecting Lies and Deceit: The Psychology of Lying and the Implications for Professional Practice* (Wiley, 2000).

Waldron, J., 'Lucky in your judge', *Theoretical Inquiries in Law*, 9:1 (January 2008), 185–216.

Webley, L., Abrams, P. and Bacquet, S., *Evaluation of Birmingham Fast and Multi Track Mediation Scheme* (Department for Constitutional Affairs, 2006).

Welsh, N., 'Making deals in court-connected mediation: what's justice got to do with it?', *Washington University Law Quarterly*, 79 (2001), 787–860.

Woo, M.K. and Wang, Y., 'Civil justice in China: An empirical study of courts in three provinces', *American Journal of Comparative Law*, 53 (2005), 911.

Woolf, The Rt Hon. Lord, *Access to Justice: Interim Report to the Lord Chancellor on the Civil Justice System in England and Wales* (HMSO, 1995).

Woolf, The Rt Hon. Lord, *The Pursuit of Justice* (Oxford University Press, 2008).

Wright, T., 'Australia: a need for clarity', *Justice System Journal*, Special Issue on Understanding Civil Justice Reform in Anglo–American Legal Systems, 20 (1999), 131.

Yeazell, S.C., 'Getting what we asked for, getting what we paid for, and not liking what we got: the vanishing civil trial', *Journal of Empirical Legal Studies*, 1:3 (2004), 943–71.

Zander, M., *The State of Justice*, Hamlyn Lectures 51st Series (Sweet and Maxwell, 2000).

Zuckerman, A.A.S., 'Justice in crisis: comparative aspects of civil procedure' in A.A.S. Zuckerman (ed.), *Civil Justice in Crisis: Comparative Aspects of Civil Procedure* (Oxford University Press, 1999).

Zuckerman, A.A.S., *Civil Procedure* (LexisNexis Butterworths, 2003).

Zuckerman, A.A.S. and Cranston, R. (eds), *The Reform of Civil Procedure: Essays on Access to Justice* (Clarendon Press, 1996).

shadow of law 21, 35
social and economic values 18–19
social change 17
social justice 89
social significance 19–20, 42, 76–7, 78
social stability 3, 78
Solum, Lawrence 14–15
substantive justice
  civil procedure 13, 14
  efficiency compared 68, 69
  mediation compared 113, 116–18, 122
  procedural justice 15, 68
  review reports 68
  rights 11, 13
Susskind, Richard 37

Thomas, LJ 45, 47

United States
  costs 32
  greedy lawyers 31

jaundiced view 31, 43
judiciary 135, 156–7
rights narrative 30–3
tort remedies 30
vanishing trial 29–30, 32

Waldron, Jeremy 160
Woolf, Lord
  anecdotal evidence 64
  civil justice safeguards 17
  Final Report (1996) 58, 93–4, 96
  Interim Report (1995) 53, 58, 64, 92
  judiciary 147
  mediation 93–6, 106
  review reports 27 -8, 52, 64–5, 67
  rule simplification 52
  settlement/diversion 53, 55
  see also review reports
Wright, Ted 59

Zander, Michael 8, 10
Zuckerman, Adrian 16, 23, 28